Contents

Lorelei the Ladybug 2
Out of the Box Friends 4
Bunny Egg Cozy 9
Buddy Bear 10
Holiday Penguin 12
Little Bo Sheep 15
Pablo Panda 18
Scholar Owl 20
Sallie Sloth 22
Black Cat Door Stop 25
Aaron Alien 27
Georgia the Giraffe 30
Olivia Octopus 32
Genie the Ghost 34
Leo the Lion 36
Bryan Bookworm 40
Paula Puppy 42
Mini Frog, Parrot, and Duck 45
Bunny Bride and Groom 48
Little Lamb Easter Egg Cozy 51
Terry the Turtle 52
Florence the Flamingo 54
Graduation Bear 58
Heather the Hippo 60
Bon Bon Magnets 64

4

12   20

32

36

45

54

Lorelei the Ladybug

Easy

MEASUREMENTS
Approx 2"/5 cm tall

MATERIALS
YARN
LION BRAND® Vanna's Choice®, 3.5 oz/100g balls, each approx 170 yd/156m (acrylic/rayon) (4)
• 1 ball each in #113 Scarlet (A), #153 Black (B)

HOOK
• One size G-6 (4 mm)

NOTIONS
• Stitch marker
• Tapestry needle
• 2 plastic safety eyes, 6 mm diameter
• Fiberfill stuffing

GAUGE
Exact gauge is not needed for this project.

NOTE
Work in continuous rnds; do not join or turn unless otherwise instructed.

LADYBUG
UPPER BODY
With A, ch 2.

Rnd 1 Work 6 sc in first ch. Place marker in first st for beg of rnd; move marker up as each rnd is completed.

Rnd 2 2 sc in each st around—12 sts.

Rnd 3 *2 sc in next st, sc in next st; rep from * around—18 sts.

Rnd 4 *2 sc in next st, sc in next 2 sts; rep from * around—24 sts.

Rnd 5 *2 sc in next st, sc in next 3 sts; rep from * around—30 sts.

Rnd 6 *2 sc in next st, sc in next 4 sts; rep from * around—36 sts.

Rnd 7 *2 sc in next st, sc in next 5 sts; rep from * around—42 sts.

Rnds 8-16 Sc in each st around.
Fasten off.

BASE
With B, ch 2.

Rnds 1-8 Work Rnds 1-8 of Upper Body—42 sts.
Fasten off.

HEAD
With B, ch 2.

Rnds 1-4 Work Rnds 1-4 of Upper Body—24 sts.

Rnds 5-8 Sc in each st around.

Rnd 9 *Sc2tog, sc in next 2 sts; rep from * around—18 sts.
Fasten off.

LEG
(Make 6)
With B, ch 2.

Rnd 1 Work 4 sc in first ch. Place marker to indicate beg of rnd; move marker up as each rnd is completed.

Rnd 2 2 sc in each st around—8 sts.

Rnds 3 and 4 Sc in each st around.
Fasten off.

SPOT
(Make 6)
With B, ch 2.

Rnds 1 and 2 Work Rnds 1 and 2 of Upper Body—12 sts.
Fasten off.

FINISHING

Following package directions, attach safety eyes to Head. Stuff Upper Body and sew to Base. Stuff Head and sew to Body. Stuff Legs very lightly and sew 3 to each side of Body at Base. Sew on Spots.

With A, embroider a straight st mouth and make 2 antennae, each about 1"/2.5 cm long on top of Head. Weave in ends. •

Out of the Box Friends

Easy

MEASUREMENTS
Approx 9"/23 cm tall

MATERIALS
YARN
Boyfriend
LION BRAND® Vanna's Choice®, 3.5oz/100g balls, each approx 17 yd/156m (acrylic/rayon) (4)
• 1 ball each in #175 Radiant Lime (A), #102 Aqua (B), #149 Silver Grey (C), #113 Scarlet (D), #130 Honey (E)

Girlfriend
LION BRAND® Vanna's Choice®, 3.5oz/100g balls, each approx 170yd/156m (acrylic/rayon) (4)
• 1 ball each in #102 Aqua (A), #113 Scarlet (B), #158 Mustard (C), #175 Radiant Lime (D), #149 Silver Grey (E), #123 Beige (F)

HOOK
• One size G-6 (4 mm)

NOTIONS
• Stitch marker
• Tapestry needle
• 4 plastic safety eyes, 9 mm diameter
• Fiberfill stuffing

GAUGE
Exact gauge is not needed for this project.

NOTES
1) Work in continuous rnds; do not join or turn unless otherwise instructed.
2) To change color, work last st of old color to last yarn over. Yarn over with new color and draw through all loops to complete st. Carry color not in use up inside of piece.

BOYFRIEND
HEAD AND BODY
With A, ch 2.

Rnd 1 Work 8 sc in first ch. Place marker in first st for beg of rnd; move marker up as each rnd is completed.

Rnd 2 2 sc in each sc around—16 sts.

Rnd 3 *2 sc in next sc, sc in next sc; rep from * around—24 sts.

Rnd 4 *2 sc in next sc, sc in next 2 sc; rep from * around—32 sts.

Rnd 5 *2 sc in next sc, sc in next 3 sc; rep from * around—40 sts.

Rnds 6-15 Sc in each sc around.

Rnd 16 Sc2tog around—20 sc.

Rnd 17 Sc in each st around.

Rnd 18 2 sc in first sc, sc in next 8 sc, 2 sc in each of next 2 sc, sc in next 8 sc, 2 sc in last sc—24 sts.

Rnd 19 2 sc in first sc, sc in next 10 sc, 2 sc in each of next 2 sc, sc in next 10 sc, 2 sc in last sc—28 sts.

Rnd 20 2 sc in first sc, sc in next 12 sc, 2 sc in each of next 2 sc, sc in next 12 sc, 2 sc in last sc—32 sts.

Rnd 21 2 sc in first sc, sc in next 14 sc, 2 sc in each of next 2 sc, sc in next 14 sc, 2 sc in last sc—36 sts.

Rnds 22-32 Sc in each st around.

Fasten off, leaving a long yarn tail for sewing.

NOSE
With B, ch 2.

Rnd 1 Work 5 sc in first ch. Place marker in first st for beg of rnd; move marker up as each rnd is completed.

Rnd 2 2 sc in each st around—10 sts.

Rnd 3 Sc in each st around.

Stuff Nose.

Rnd 4 Sc2tog around—5 sts.

Fasten off.

EAR

(Make 2)

With C, ch 6.

Row 1 Sc in third ch from hook, 2 dc in next ch, hdc in next ch, (sc, ch 2, sc) in last ch; working along opposite side of foundation ch, hdc in next ch, 2 dc in next ch. Fasten off.

ARM

(Make 2)

With E, ch 2.

Rnd 1 Work 6 sc in first ch. Place marker in first st for beg of rnd; move marker up as each rnd is completed.

Rnds 2–12 Sc in each sc around. Fasten off.

LEG

(Make 2)

With C, ch 2.

Rnd 1 Work 8 sc in first ch. Place marker in first st for beg of rnd; move marker up as each rnd is completed.

Rnd 2 Sc in each sc around, changing to D in last st.

Rnds 3 and 4 Sc in each sc around, changing to C in last st of Rnd 4.

Continue in this way, working 2 rnds with C and D alternately, until you've completed 18 rnds. Fasten off.

FINISHING

Following package instructions, attach eyes to face. Sew Nose and Ears to Head. With D, embroider a straight st smile. Stuff Head and Body firmly, then sew closed. Stuff Arms and Legs and sew to Body.

Weave in ends.

Out of the Box Friends

BOX
FRONT/BACK
(Make 2)

With E, ch 21.

Row 1 Sc in second ch from hook and in each ch across—20 sts.

Rows 2-16 Ch 1, turn, sc in each sc across. Fasten off.

SIDE
(Make 2)

With E, ch 9.

Row 1 Sc in second ch from hook and in each ch across—8 sts.

Rows 2-12 Ch 1, turn, sc in each sc across.

Armhole
Row 13 Ch 1, turn, sc in first 3 sts, ch 2, sk 2 sts, sc in last 3 sts.

Row 14 Ch 1, turn, sc in each sc and ch across—8 sts.

Rows 15 and 16 Ch 1, turn, sc in each sc across. Fasten off.

BASE
With E, ch 21.

Row 1 Sc in second ch from hook and in each ch across—20 sts.

Rows 2-4 Ch 1, turn, sc in each sc across—20 sts.

Make Leg Openings.

Row 5 Ch 1, turn, sc in first 4 sts, ch 3, sk 3 sts, sc in next 6 sts, ch 3, sk 3 sts, sc to end.

Row 6 Ch 1, turn, sc in each sc and ch across—20 sts.

Rows 7 and 8 Ch 1, turn, sc in each sc across. Fasten off.

TOP
With E, ch 21.

Row 1 Sc in second ch from hook and in each ch across—20 sts.

Rows 2-4 Ch 1, turn, sc in each sc across. Fasten off.

FINISHING
From RS with E, work sc evenly spaced through both thicknesses to join Front, Back, and Sides to make a 4-sided box.

The end of the Box that Armholes are closest to is the top of the Box.

From RS with E, work sc evenly spaced through both thicknesses to join Base to bottom of Box. In same way, join one long side of top to one long edge of Box.

Slip Boyfriend into Box, bringing Arms out through Armholes.

Weave in ends.

GIRLFRIEND
HEAD AND BODY
With A, ch 2.

Rnd 1 Work 8 sc in first ch. Place marker in first st for beg of rnd; move marker up as each rnd is completed.

Rnd 2 2 sc in each sc around—16 sc.

Rnd 3 *2 sc in next sc, sc in next sc; rep from * around—24 sts.

Rnd 4 *2 sc in next sc, sc in next 2 sc; rep from * around—32 sts.

Rnd 5 *2 sc in next sc, sc in next 3 sc; rep from * around—40 sts.

Rnds 6-15 Sc in each sc around.

Rnd 16 Sc2tog around—20 sc.

Rnd 17 Sc in each sc around.

Rnd 18 2 sc in first sc, sc in next 8 sc, 2 sc in each of next 2 sc, sc in next 8 sc, 2 sc in last sc—24 sts.

Rnd 19 2 sc in first sc, sc in next 10 sc, 2 sc in each of next 2 sc, sc in next 10 sc, 2 sc in last sc—28 sts.

Rnd 20 2 sc in first sc, sc in next 12 sc, 2 sc in each of next 2 sc, sc in next 12 sc, 2 sc in last sc—32 sts.

Rnd 21 2 sc in first sc, sc in next 14 sc, 2 sc in each of next 2 sc, sc in next 14 sc, 2 sc in last sc—36 sts.

Rnds 22-32 Sc in each sc around.

Fasten off, leaving a long yarn tail for sewing.

NOSE
With B, ch 2.

Rnd 1 Work 5 sc in first ch. Place marker in first st for beg of rnd; move marker up as each rnd is completed.

Rnd 2 2 sc in each sc around—10 sts.

Rnd 3 Sc in each sc around.

Stuff Nose.

Rnd 4 Sc2tog around—5 sts.

Fasten off.

HAIR
With D, ch 2.

Rnds 1-5 Work Rnds 1-5 of Head and Body.

Rnds 6-8 Sc in each sc around.

Rnds 9-11 Hdc in next 17 sts, sc in next 3 sts, sl st in next st, sc in next 3 sts, hdc in next 16 sts.

Fasten off.

EAR
(Make 2)

With C, ch 6.

Row 1 Sc in third ch from hook, 2 dc in next ch, hdc in next ch, (sc, ch 2, sc) in last ch; working along opposite side of foundation ch, hdc in next ch, 2 dc in next ch.

Fasten off.

ARM
(Make 2)

With E, ch 2.

Rnd 1 Work 6 sc in first ch. Place marker in first st for beg of rnd; move marker up as each rnd is completed.

Rnds 2-12 Sc in each sc around.

Fasten off.

LEG
(Make 2)

With E, ch 2.

Rnd 1 Work 8 sc in first ch. Place marker in first st for beg of rnd; move marker up as each rnd is completed.

Rnd 2 Sc in each sc around, changing to C in last st.

Rnds 3 and 4 Sc in each sc around, changing to E in last st of Rnd 4.

Continue in this way, working 2 rnds with C and E alternately, until you've completed 18 rnds.

Fasten off.

FINISHING
Following package instructions, attach safety eyes to face. Sew Nose and Ears to Head. With D, embroider a straight st smile. Stuff Head and Body firmly, then sew closed. Stuff Arms and Legs and sew to Body.

Sew Hair to Head. Weave in ends.

Braids
Cut 6 strands of D 16"/40.5 cm long. Draw 3 strands through one side of Head, drawing ends of strands out evenly so that you have 6 strands. Divide into 3 groups of 2 strands each and braid. Wrap end of braid with a short length of yarn; trim ends of braids.

Out of the Box Friends

BOX

FRONT/BACK

(Make 2)

With F, ch 17.

Row 1 Sc in second ch from hook and in each ch across—16 sts.

Rows 2-16 Ch 1, turn, sc in each sc across. Fasten off.

SIDE

(Make 2)

With F, ch 9.

Row 1 Sc in second ch from hook and in each ch across—8 sts.

Rows 2-12 Ch 1, turn, sc in each sc across—8 sts.

Armhole

Row 13 Ch 1, turn, sc in first 3 sts, ch 2, sk 2 sts, sc in last 3 sts.

Row 14 Ch 1, turn, sc in each sc and ch across—8 sts.

Rows 15 and 16 Ch 1, turn, sc in each sc across. Fasten off.

FRONT/BACK FLAP

(Make 2)

With F, ch 17.

Row 1 Sc in second ch from hook and in each ch across—16 sts.

Rows 2-4 Ch 1, turn, sc in each sc across—16 sts. Fasten off.

SIDE FLAP

(Make 2)

With F, ch 9.

Row 1 Sc in second ch from hook and in each ch across—8 sts.

Rows 2-4 Ch 1, turn, sc in each sc across. Fasten off.

FINISHING

From RS with F, work sc evenly spaced through both thicknesses to join Front, Back, and Sides to make a 4-sided Box.

The end of the Box that Armholes are closest to is the top of the Box.

Sew one long edge of each flap to corresponding section at lower edge of Box.

Slip Girlfriend into Box, bringing Arms through armholes. Weave in ends. •

Bunny Egg Cozy

Easy

MATERIALS

YARN

LION BRAND® Wool-Ease®, 3oz/85g balls, each approx 197yd/180m (acrylic/wool)

- 1 ball each in #099 Fisherman (A), #104 Blush Heather (B)

HOOK

- One size G-6 (4 mm)

NOTIONS

- Stitch marker
- Tapestry needle
- Small black beads
- Pom-pom maker

GAUGE

Exact gauge is not needed for this project.

NOTES

Work in continuous rnds; do not join or turn unless otherwise instructed.

COZY

With A, ch 2.

Rnd 1 Work 4 sc in first ch. Place marker in first st for beg of rnd; move marker up as each rnd is completed.

Rnd 2 Work 2 sc in each sc around—8 sc.

Rnd 3 *2 sc in next st, sc in next st, rep from * around—12 sc.

Rnd 4 *2 sc in next st, sc in each of next 2 sts, rep from * around—16 sts.

Rnd 5 *2 sc in next st, sc in each of next 3 sts, rep from * around—20 sts.

Rnd 6 *2 sc in next st, sc in each of next 4 sts, rep from * around—24 sts.

Rnds 7-14 Sc in each sc around.

Rnd 15 *Sc2tog, sc in each of next 2 sts, rep from * around. Fasten off.

EAR

(Make 2)

With A, ch 2.

Rnd 1 Work 4 sc in first ch. Place marker in first st for beg of rnd; move marker up as each rnd is completed.

Rnd 2 *2 sc in next st, sc in next st, rep from * around—6 sc.

Rnd 3 *2 sc in next st, sc in each of next 2 sts, rep from * around—8 sts.

Rnds 4-8 Sc in each st around. Fasten off.

FINISHING

Sew beads onto face for eyes. With B, embroider straight st triangle for nose. Lightly stuff Ears and sew to Cozy. Following package directions, make a small pom-pom for tail. Sew tail to Cozy. Weave in ends. •

Buddy Bear

Easy

MEASUREMENTS
Approx 14"/35.5 cm tall

MATERIALS
YARN
LION BRAND® Homespun®, 6oz/170g balls, each approx 185yd/169m (acrylic/polyester) (5)
- 1 ball in #403 Earth
- Small amount of black yarn

HOOK
- One size H-8 (5 mm)

NOTIONS
- Stitch marker
- Tapestry needle
- 2 plastic safety eyes, 12 mm diameter
- Fiberfill stuffing

GAUGE
Exact gauge is not needed for this project.

NOTE
Work in continuous rnds; do not join or turn unless otherwise instructed.

BEAR
HEAD
Ch 2.

Rnd 1 Work 6 sc in second ch from hook. Place marker in first st for beg of rnd; move marker up as each rnd is completed.

Rnd 2 2 sc in each st around—12 sts.

Rnd 3 (2 sc in next st, sc in next st) 6 times—18 sts.

Rnd 4 (2 sc in next st, sc in next 2 sts) 6 times—24 sts.

Rnd 5 (2 sc in next st, sc in next 3 sts) 6 times—30 sts.

Rnd 6 (2 sc in next st, sc in next 4 sts) 6 times—36 sts.

Rnds 7-15 Sc in each st around.

Rnd 16 (Sc2tog, sc in next 4 sts) 6 times—30 sts.

Rnd 17 (Sc2tog, sc in next 3 sts) 6 times—24 sts.

Rnd 18 (Sc2tog, sc in next 2 sts) 6 times—18 sts.
Fasten off.

BODY
Ch 2.

Rnds 1-5 Work Rnds 1-5 of Head—30 sts.

Rnd 6 Sc in next 14 sc, 2 sc in each of next 2 sc, sc in next 14 sc—32 sts.

Rnd 7 Sc in next 15 sc, 2 sc in each of next 2 sc, sc in next 15 sc—34 sts.

Rnd 8 Sc in next 16 sc, 2 sc in each of next 2 sc, sc in next 16 sc—36 sts.

Rnds 9-14 Sc in each st around.

Rnd 15 Sc in next 16 sts, (sc2tog) twice, sc in next 16 sts—34 sts.

Rnd 16 Sc in next 15 sts, (sc2tog) twice, sc in next 15 sts—32 sts.

Rnd 17 Sc in next 14 sts, (sc2tog) twice, sc in next 14 sts—30 sts.

Rnd 18 Sc in next 13 sts, (sc2tog) twice, sc in next 13 sts—28 sts.

Rnd 19 Sc in next 12 sts, (sc2tog) twice, sc in next 12 sts—26 sts.

Rnd 20 Sc in next 11 sts, (sc2tog) twice, sc in next 11 sts—24 sts.

Rnd 21 (Sc2tog, sc in next 2 sts) 6 times—18 sts.
Fasten off.

EAR

(Make 2)

Ch 2.

Rnds 1-3 Work Rnds 1-3 of Head—18 sts. Fasten off.

ARM

(Make 2)

Ch 2.

Rnds 1 and 2 Work Rnds 1 and 2 of Head—12 sts.

Rnd 3 Sc in each st around.

Rnd 4 Sc2tog, sc in next 8 sts, sc2tog—10 sts.

Rnds 5-14 Sc in each st around. Fasten off.

LEG

(Make 2)

Ch 2.

Rnds 1-3 Work Rnds 1-3 of Head—18 sts.

Rnds 4 and 5 Sc in each st around.

Rnd 6 Sc2tog, sc in next 14 sts, sc2tog—16 sts.

Rnd 7 Sc2tog, sc in next 12 sts, sc2tog—14 sts.

Rnds 8-18 Sc in each st around. Fasten off.

FINISHING

Following package directions, attach safety eyes to Head. Firmly stuff Head. With black yarn, embroider straight st nose. Fold Ears in half to make semicircles and sew closed. Sew Ears to Head. Firmly stuff Body, sew Head to Body. Stuff Arms and Legs lightly and sew to Body. Weave in ends. •

Holiday Penguin

Easy

MEASUREMENTS
Approx 9"/23 cm tall

MATERIALS
YARN
LION BRAND® Vanna's Choice®, 3.5oz/100g balls, each approx 170yd/156m (acrylic/rayon) (4)
- 1 ball each in #153 Black (A), #100 White (B), #158 Mustard (C), #133 Brick (D), #174 Olive (E)

HOOK
- One size G-6 (4 mm)

NOTIONS
- Stitch marker
- Tapestry needle
- 2 plastic safety eyes, 9 mm diameter
- Fiberfill stuffing

GAUGE
Exact gauge is not needed for this project.

NOTE
Work in continuous rnds; do not join or turn unless otherwise instructed.

PENGUIN
HEAD
With A, ch 2.

Rnd 1 Work 6 sc in first ch. Place marker in first st for beg of rnd; move marker up as each rnd is completed.

Rnd 2 2 sc in each sc around—12 sts.

Rnd 3 *2 sc in next sc, sc in next sc; rep from * around—18 sts.

Rnd 4 *2 sc in next sc, sc in each of next 2 sc; rep from * around—24 sts.

Rnd 5 *2 sc in next sc, sc in each of next 3 sc; rep from * around—30 sts.

Rnd 6 *2 sc in next sc, sc in each of next 4 sc; rep from * around—36 sts.

Rnds 7-13 Sc in each sc around.

Fasten off A.

Rnd 14 With B, sc in each sc around—36 sts.

Rnd 15 *Sc2tog, sc in each of next 4 sc; rep from * around—30 sts.

Rnd 16 *Sc2tog, sc in each of next 3 sc; rep from * around—24 sts.

Rnd 17 *Sc2tog, sc in each of next 2 sc; rep from * around—18 sts.

Fasten off.

BODY
With A, ch 2.

Rnds 1-6 Work Rnds 1-6 of Head.

Rnd 7 *2 sc in next sc, sc in each of next 5 sc; rep from * around—42 sts.

Rnd 8 *2 sc in next sc, sc in each of next 6 sc; rep from * around—48 sts.

Rnds 9-19 Sc in each sc around.

Rnd 20 *Sc2tog, sc in each of next 6 sc; rep from * around—42 sts.

Rnd 21 *Sc2tog, sc in each of next 5 sc; rep from * around—36 sts.

Rnd 22 *Sc2tog, sc in each of next 4 sc; rep from * around—30 sts.

Rnd 23 *Sc2tog, sc in each of next 3 sc; rep from * around—24 sts.

Rnd 24 *Sc2tog, sc in each of next 2 sc; rep from * around—18 sts.

Fasten off.

EYE

(Make 2)

With B, ch 2.

Rnd 1 Work 6 sc in first ch. Place marker in first st for beg of rnd; move marker up as each rnd is completed.

Rnd 2 2 sc in each sc around—12 sts.

Fasten off.

BEAK

With C, ch 2.

Rnd 1 Work 3 sc in first ch. Place marker in first st for beg of rnd; move marker up as each rnd is completed.

Rnd 2 2 sc in each sc around—6 sts.

Rnd 3 *2 sc in next sc, sc in next sc; rep from * around—9 sts.

Rnd 4 *2 sc in next sc, sc in each of next 2 sc; rep from * around—12 sts.

Fasten off.

FOOT

(Make 2)

With C, ch 2.

Rnd 1 Work 6 sc in first ch. Place marker in first st for beg of rnd; move marker up as each rnd is completed.

13

Holiday Penguin

Rnd 2 2 sc in each sc around—12 sts.

Rnds 3 and 4 Sc in each sc around.

Fasten off.

WING

(Make 2)

With A, ch 2.

Rnd 1 Work 4 sc in first ch. Place marker in first st for beg of rnd; move marker up as each rnd is completed.

Rnd 2 2 sc in each sc around—8 sts.

Rnd 3 *2 sc in next sc, sc in next sc; rep from * around—12 sts.

Rnds 4-13 Sc in each sc around.

Rnd 14 *Sc2tog, sc in next sc; rep from * around—8 sts.

Fasten off.

TUMMY PATCH

With B, ch 2.

Rnd 1 Work 6 sc in first ch. Place marker in first st for beg of rnd; move marker up as each rnd is completed.

Rnd 2 2 sc in each sc around—12 sts.

Rnd 3 *2 sc in next sc, sc in next sc; rep from * around—18 sts.

Rnd 4 *2 sc in next sc, sc in each of next 2 sc; rep from * around—24 sts.

Rnd 5 Sc in next 11 sc, 2 dc in each of next 2 sc, sc in next 11 sc.

Fasten off.

SCARF

With E, ch 5.

Row 1 Sc in second ch from hook and each ch across—4 sts.

Row 2 Ch 1, turn. Sc in each sc across.

Rep Row 2 until scarf measures 12"/30.5 cm from beg.

Fasten off.

HAT

With D, ch 2.

Rnd 1 Work 6 sc in first ch. Place marker in first st for beg of rnd; move marker up as each rnd is completed.

Rnd 2 2 sc in each sc around—12 sts.

Rnds 3 and 4 Sc in each sc around.

Rnd 5 Sc2tog around—6 sts.

Rnd 6 With E, sc in each sc around.

Rnd 7 *2 sc in next sc, sc in next sc; rep from * around—9 sts.

Rnd 8 With D, sc in each sc around.

Rnd 9 *2 sc in next sc, sc in each of next 2 sc; rep from * around—12 sts.

Rnd 10 With E, sc in each sc around.

Rnd 11 *2 sc in next sc, sc in each of next 3 sc; rep from * around—15 sts.

Rnd 12 With D, sc in each sc around.

Rnd 13 *2 sc in next sc, sc in each of next 4 sc; rep from * around—18 sts.

Rnd 14 With E, sc in each sc around.

Rnd 15 *2 sc in next sc, sc in each of next 5 sc; rep from * around—21 sts.

Rnd 16 With D, sc in each sc around.

Rnd 17 *2 sc in next sc, sc in each of next 6 sc; rep from * around—24 sts.

Rnd 18 With E, sc in each sc around.

Rnd 19 *2 sc in next sc, sc in each of next 7 sc; rep from * around—27 sts.

Rnd 20 With D, sc in each sc around.

Rnd 21 *2 sc in next sc, sc in each of next 8 sc; rep from * around—30 sts.

Fasten off.

FINISHING

Following package directions, attach safety eyes to crocheted Eyes. Sew Eyes to Head. Stuff Head and Body firmly. Sew Head to Body, sew on Tummy Patch and Beak. Sew Wings and Feet to each side.

Lightly stuff Hat and sew to Head, fold down Hat, and tack down. Tie Scarf around neck. Weave in ends. •

Little Bo Sheep

Easy

MEASUREMENTS
About 8.5"/21.5 cm wide, 6"/15 cm tall

MATERIALS
YARN
LION BRAND® Feels Like Butta®, 3.5 oz/100 g balls, each approx 55 yd/50 m (polyester) (6)
- 1 ball in #150 Charcoal (A)

LION BRAND® Go For Faux®, 3.5 oz/100 g balls, each approx. 65 yd/60 m (polyester) (6)
- 1 ball in #302 Star (B)

HOOKS
- One G-6 (4 mm) and one size H-8 (5 mm)

NOTIONS
- Stitch markers
- Tapestry needle
- 2 safety eyes, 10 mm diameter
- Fiberfill stuffing

GAUGE
24 sc = about 4"/10 cm with smaller hook and A.
Exact gauge is not needed for this project.

NOTES
1) Sheep is made in 8 pieces—Head, 2 Ears, Body, and 4 Legs.
2) Pieces are stuffed, then sewn together.
3) Work in continuous rnds; do not join or turn unless otherwise instructed.
4) We worked tightly with a small hook so that stuffing does not show through spaces between stitches.

SHEEP
HEAD
With smaller hook and A, ch 13.

Rnd 1 (RS) Sc in second ch from hook, sc in next 10 ch, 3 sc in last ch; working along opposite side of foundation ch, sc in next 10 ch, 3 sc in next ch. Place marker in

Little Bo Sheep

first st for beg of rnd; move marker up as each rnd is completed—27 sts.

Rnd 2 Sc in next 11 sts, 2 sc in next 3 sts, sc in next 10 sts, 2 sc in next 3 sts—33 sts.

Rnds 3-10 Sc in each st around.

Rnd 11 Sc2tog, sc in next 11 sts, sc2tog, sc in next 2 sts, sc2tog, sc in next 10 sts, sc2tog, sc in next 2 sts—29 sts.

Rnds 12-18 Sc in each st around.

Fasten off A.

Attach safety eyes between Rnds 14 and 15, about 3 sts apart.

Top of Head

Rnd 19 With larger hook, join B with sc in first st, sc in next st, *sk next st, sc in next 2 sts; rep from * around; join with sl st in first sc—20 sts.

Rnd 20 Ch 1, sc in each st around; join with sl st in first sc. Fasten off, leaving a long yarn tail.

Stuff Head.

Thread yarn tail through top of sts of last rnd. Pull tail to close opening and knot.

BODY

With larger hook and B, ch 2.

Rnd 1 Work 10 sc in second ch from hook. Place marker in first st for beg of rnd; move marker up as each rnd is completed—10 sts.

Rnd 2 Work 2 sc in each st around—20 sts.

Rnd 3 *Sc in next st, 2 sc in next st; rep from * around—30 sts.

Rnds 4-11 Sc in each st around.

Rnd 12 *Sc in next 2 sts, sk next st; rep from * around—20 sts.

Rnd 13 Sc in each st around.

Rnd 14 *Sc in next st, sk next st; rep from * around—10 sts.

Fasten off, leaving a long yarn tail.

Stuff Body.

Thread yarn tail through top of sts of last rnd. Pull tail to close opening and knot.

EAR

(Make 2)

With smaller hook and A, ch 2.

Rnd 1 Work 4 sc in second ch from hook. Place marker in first st for beg of rnd; move marker up as each rnd is completed.

Rnd 2 Work 2 sc in each st around—8 sts.

Rnd 3 Sc in each st around.

Rnd 4 *Sc in next st, 2 sc in next st; rep from * around—12 sts.

Rnd 5 *Sc in next 2 sts, 2 sc in next st; rep from * around—16 sts.

Rnds 6 and 7 Sc in each st around.

Rnd 8 * Sc in next 2 sts, sc2tog; rep from * around—12 sts.

Rnds 9 and 10 Sc in each st around.

Fasten off, leaving a long tail for sewing.

LEG

(Make 4)

With smaller hook and A, ch 2.

Rnd 1 Work 6 sc in second ch from hook; join with sl st in first sc—6 sts.

Rnd 2 Ch 1, 2 sc in each st around; join with sl st in first sc—12 sts.

Rnd 3 Ch 1, * sc in next st, 2 sc in next st; rep from * around; join with sl st in first sc—18 sts.

Rnd 4 Ch 1, *working in the back loops only*, * sc in next 2 sts, 2 sc in next st; rep from * around. Place marker in first st for beg of rnd; move marker up as each rnd is completed—24 sts.

Rnd 5 Sc in each st around.

Rnd 6 *Sc in next 2 sts, sc2tog; rep from * around—18 sts.

Rnd 7 *Sc in next st, sc2tog; rep from * around—12 sts.

Rnds 8 and 9 Sc in each st around.

Fasten off, leaving a long tail for sewing.

FINISHING

Sew Head to Body and Ears to Head.

Stuff Legs and sew to Body.

Weave in ends. ●

Pablo Panda

Easy

MEASUREMENTS
Approx 5"/13 cm tall

MATERIALS
YARN
LION BRAND® Vanna's Choice®, 3.5oz/100g balls, each approx 170yd/156m (acrylic/rayon)
• 1 ball each in #100 White (A), #153 Black (B)

HOOK
• One size G-6 (4 mm)

NOTIONS
• Stitch marker
• Tapestry needle
• 2 plastic safety eyes, 9 mm diameter
• Fiberfill stuffing

GAUGE
Exact gauge is not needed for this project.

NOTE
Work in continuous rnds; do not join or turn unless otherwise instructed.

PANDA
EYE
(Make 2)

With B, ch 2.

Rnd 1 Work 8 sc in first ch. Place marker in first st for beg of rnd; move marker up as each rnd is completed.

Rnd 2 Work 2 sc in each sc around—16 sts.

Fasten off.

HEAD AND BODY
With A, ch 2.

Rnd 1 Work 6 sc in first ch. Place marker in first st for beg of rnd; move marker up as each rnd is completed.

Rnd 2 Work 2 sc in each st around—12 sts.

Rnd 3 *2 sc in next st, sc in next st, rep from * around—18 sts.

Rnd 4 *2 sc in next st, sc in each of next 2 sts, rep from * around—24 sts.

Rnd 5 *2 sc in next st, sc in each of next 3 sts, rep from * around—30 sts.

Rnd 6 *2 sc in next st, sc in each of next 4 sts, rep from * around—36 sts.

Rnd 7 *2 sc in next st, sc in each of next 5 sts, rep from * around—42 sts.

Rnds 8-12 Sc in each st around.

Sew Eyes to Body, leaving about .75"/2 cm between Eyes. Following package directions, attach safety eyes through center of each crocheted Eye.

Change to B.

Rnds 13-15 Sc in each st around. Change to A.

Rnd 16 and 17 Sc in each st around.

Rnd 18 *Sc2tog, sc in each of next 5 sts, rep from * around—36 sts.

Rnd 19 *Sc2tog, sc in each of next 4 sts, rep from * around—30 sts.

Stuff piece firmly. Continue stuffing as work progresses.

Rnd 20 *Sc2tog, sc in each of next 3 sts, rep from * around—24 sts.

Rnd 21 *Sc2tog, sc in each of next 2 sts, rep from * around—18 sts.

Rnd 22 *Sc2tog, sc in next st, rep from * around—12 sts.

Rnd 23 (Sc2tog) around—6 sts.

Fasten off.

ARM/LEG

(Make 4)

With B, ch 2.

Rnd 1 Work 8 sc in first ch. Place marker in first st for beg of rnd; move marker up as each rnd is completed.

Rnds 2-5 Sc in each st around—8 sts.

Fasten off.

EAR

(Make 2)

With B, ch 2.

Rnd 1 Work 8 sc in first ch. Place marker in first st for beg of rnd; move marker up as each rnd is completed.

Rnds 2 and 3 Sc in each sc around—8 sts.

Rnd 4 (Sc2tog) around—4 sts.

Fasten off.

FINISHING

With B, embroider straight st nose and mouth on Head.

Lightly stuff Ears, Arms, and Legs and sew to Body.

Weave in ends. •

Scholar Owl

Easy

MEASUREMENTS
Approx 6"/15 cm tall

MATERIALS
YARN
LION BRAND® Vanna's Choice®, 3.5oz/100g balls, each approx 170yd/156m (acrylic/rayon)

• 1 ball each in #126 Chocolate (A), #099 Linen (B), #100 White (C), #158 Mustard (D), #110 Navy (E)

HOOK
• One size G-6 (4 mm)

NOTIONS
• Stitch marker
• Tapestry needle
• 2 plastic safety eyes, 9 mm diameter
• Fiberfill stuffing

GAUGE
Exact gauge is not needed for this project.

NOTE
Work in continuous rnds; do not join rnds or turn unless otherwise instructed.

OWL
HEAD
With A, ch 2.

Rnd 1 Work 6 sc in first ch. Place marker in first st for beg of rnd; move marker up as each rnd is completed.

Rnd 2 2 sc in each st around—12 sts.

Rnd 3 *2 sc in next st, sc in next st; rep from * around—18 sts.

Rnd 4 *2 sc in next st, sc in next 2 sts; rep from * around—24 sts.

Rnd 5 *2 sc in next st, sc in next 3 sts; rep from * around—30 sts.

Rnds 6-13 Sc in each st around.

Rnd 14 *Sc2tog, sc in next 3 sts; rep from * around—24 sts.

Rnd 15 *Sc2tog, sc in next 2 sts; rep from * around—18 sts. Fasten off.

BODY
With B, ch 2.

Rnds 1-5 Work Rnds 1-5 of Head—30 sts.

Rnd 6 *2 sc in next st, sc in next 4 sts; rep from * around—36 sts.

Rnds 7-15 Sc in each st around.

Rnd 16 *Sc2tog, sc in next 4 sts; rep from * around—30 sts.

Rnd 17 *Sc2tog, sc in next 3 sts; rep from * around—24 sts.

Rnd 18 *Sc2tog, sc in next 2 sts; rep from * around—18 sts. Fasten off.

OUTER EYE
(Make 2)

With B, ch 2.

Rnds 1-3 Work Rnds 1-3 of Head—18 sts. Fasten off.

INNER EYE
(Make 2)

With C, ch 2.

Rnds 1 and 2 Work Rnds 1 and 2 of Head—12 sts. Fasten off.

WING
(Make 2)

With A, ch 2.

Rnd 1 Work 4 sc in first ch. Place marker in first st for beg of rnd; move marker up as each rnd is completed.

Rnd 2 2 sc in each st around—8 sts.

Rnd 3 *2 sc in next st, sc in next st; rep from * around—12 sts.

Rnd 4 *2 sc in next st, sc in next 2 sts; rep from * around—16 sts.

Rnds 5-11 Sc in each st around.

Rnd 12 (Sc2tog) 8 times—8 sts.

Fasten off.

BEAK

With D, ch 2.

Rnds 1 and 2 Work Rnds 1 and 2 of Wing—8 sts.

Fasten off.

EAR

(Make 1)

With A, ch 2. Make as for Beak.

CAP

With E, ch 2.

Rnds 1-4 Work Rnds 1-4 of Head—24 sts.

Rnd 5 Sc in each st around.

Fasten off.

MORTARBOARD

(Make 2)

With E, ch 9.

Row 1 Sc in second ch from hook and in each ch across—8 sts.

Rows 2-8 Ch 1, turn, sc in each st across.

Fasten off.

FOOT

(Make 2)

With A, ch 4.

Row 1 Sc in second ch from hook and in each ch across—3 sts.

Row 2 Ch 1, turn, sc in next 2 sts, 2 sc in last st—4 sts.

Row 3 Ch 1, turn, 2 sc in first st, sc in next 3 sts—5 sts.

Row 4 Ch 1, turn, sc in first 3 sts; leave rem sts unworked—3 sts.

Fasten off.

FINISHING

Layer Inner Eyes on Outer Eyes. Following package directions, insert safety eyes through center of Eyes and attach to Head.

Firmly stuff Head. Stuff Beak and sew to Head. Stuff Body firmly and sew to Head.

Sew Wings to sides of Body. With shaped edge at front, sew Feet to bottom of Body.

With WS of the 2 Mortarboards together and working through both thicknesses, join E with sl st edge and work sc evenly spaced around outside edge.

Sew Mortarboard to center of Cap, then sew hat onto one side of Head and Ear to opposite side. Sew a strand of D to top of Mortarboard for tassel, fray end of strand.

Weave in ends. •

Sallie Sloth

Easy

MEASUREMENTS
Approx 9"/23 cm high, seated

MATERIALS
YARN
LION BRAND® Go For Faux®, 3.5oz/100g balls, each approx 65yd/60m (polyester) [6]
- 2 balls in #206 Bear (A)

LION BRAND® Feels Like Butta®, 3.5oz/100g balls, each approx 55yd/50m (polyester) [6]
- 1 ball in #153 Black (B)

LION BRAND® Wool-Ease®, 3oz/85g balls, each approx 197yd/180m (acrylic/wool) [4]
- 1 ball in #098 Natural Heather (C)

HOOKS
- One size G-6 (4 mm) and one size H-8 (5 mm)

NOTIONS
- Stitch markers
- Tapestry needle
- 2 safety eyes, 12mm diameter
- Fiberfill stuffing

GAUGE
24 sc = about 4"/10 cm with smaller hook and B. See Notes.

NOTES
1) Sloth is made in one Body/Head piece. The Face, Arms, Legs, and Eye Patches are worked separately.
2) Pieces are sewn together and stuffed to make the Sloth.
3) Exact gauge isn't crucial but it is meant to be a bit tight—this helps keep the stuffing from poking through.
4) Work in continuous rnds; do not join unless otherwise indicated.

SLOTH
BODY/HEAD
Body
Beg at bottom of Body, with larger hook and A, ch 2.

Rnd 1 (RS) Work 10 sc in second ch from hook. Place marker in first st for beg of rnd; move marker up as each rnd is completed.

Rnd 2 Work 2 sc in each st around—20 sc.

Rnd 3 *Sc in next st, 2 sc in next st; rep from * around—30 sc.

Rnd 4 *Sc in next 2 sts, 2 sc in next st; rep from * around—40 sc.

Rnds 5-16 Sc in each st around.

Rnd 17 *Sc in next 3 sts, sk next st; rep from * around—30 sc.

Rnd 18 *Sc in next 2 sts, sk next st; rep from * around—20 sc.

Rnd 19 Rep Rnd 17—15 sc.

Stuff Body firmly, but do not fasten off.

Head
Rnd 20 Sc in each st around.

Rnd 21 Work 2 sc in each st around—30 sc.

Rnd 22 *Sc in next 2 sts, 2 sc in next st; rep from * around—40 sc.

Rnds 23-30 Sc in each st around.

Rnd 31 *Sc in next 3 sts, sk next st; rep from * around—30 sc.

Rnd 32 *Sc in next 2 sts, sk next st; rep from * around—20 sc.

Stuff Head firmly.

Rnds 33 and 34 *Sc in next st, sk next st; rep from * around—5 sc.

Fasten off, leaving a long yarn tail for sewing.
Stuff Head firmly.
Thread yarn tail onto needle and sew opening closed.

ARM/LEG
(Make 4)
Beg at hand or foot, with smaller hook and C, ch 2.

Rnd 1 (RS) Work 6 sc in second ch from hook. Place marker in first st for beg of rnd; move marker up as each rnd is completed.
Rnd 2 Work 2 sc in each st around—12 sc.
Rnds 3-6 Sc in each st around.
Rnd 7 Sc in each st around; join with sl st in first sc of this rnd.

Sallie Sloth

Fasten off.

Turn piece inside out so that you are looking at inside (WS) of piece. We found we preferred the look of yarn C on WS, that's why you'll now continue working on the WS.

Rnd 8 Join A with a sl st in any st, ch 1, sc in each st around. Place marker in first st for beg of rnd; move marker up as each rnd is completed.

Rnds 9-22 Sc in each st around.

Fasten off, leaving a long yarn tail for sewing.

Claws

With smaller hook, join C with a sl st around post of any st in Rnd 2. Ch 4, sl st in second ch from hook and in next 2 ch, sl st around same st in Rnd 2, sl st around post of closest st in Rnd 1, ch 4, sl st in second ch from hook and in next 2 ch, sl st around same st in Rnd 1, sl st around post of Rnd 1 st directly across from previous st, ch 4, sl st in second ch from hook and in next 2 ch, sl st around post of same st in Rnd 1.

Fasten off.

Stuff each Arm and Leg about halfway, leaving ends unstuffed.

FACE

With smaller hook and C, ch 8.

Row 1 Work 2 sc in second ch from hook and in next 5 ch, 2 sc in last ch—9 sc.

Row 2 Ch 1, turn, sc in each st across.

Rows 3 and 4 Ch 1, turn, 2 sc in first st, sc in each st to last st, 2 sc in last st—13 sc in Row 4.

Rows 5-8 Ch 1, turn, sc in each st across.

Row 9 Ch 1, turn, sc to last 2 sts, sc2tog—12 sc.

Row 10 Ch 1, turn, sc2tog, sc in each st across—11 sc.

Row 11 Rep Row 9–10 sc.

Row 12 Ch 1, turn, 2 sc in first st, sc in each st across—11 sc.

Row 13 Ch 1, turn, sc to last st, 2 sc in last st—12 sc.

Row 14 Rep Row 12–13 sc.

Rows 15-19 Ch 1, turn, sc in each st across.

Rows 20 and 21 Turn, sc2tog, sc in each st to last 2 sts, sc2tog–9 sc in Row 21.

Row 22 Ch 1, turn, sc in each st across.

Row 23 Turn, sc2tog, sc to last 2 sts, sc2tog—7 sc.

Trim

Rnd 1 Ch 1, work sl st evenly spaced around outside edge of piece; join with sl st in first sl st.

Fasten off, leaving a long yarn tail for sewing.

EYE PATCH

(Make 2)

With smaller hook and B, ch 7. Sc in second ch from hook and in next ch, hdc in next 2 ch, dc in next ch, 9 dc in last ch; working along opposite side of foundation ch, dc in next ch, hdc in next 2 ch, sc in next 2 ch; join with sl st in first sc—19 sts.

Fasten off, leaving a long yarn tail for sewing.

FINISHING

Attach a safety eye in the center of the 9-dc at end of each Eye Patch. Sew Eye Patches to Face.

Note Do not trim yarn ends after sewing Patch to Face—you can use those ends to embroider the nose and mouth. With B, embroider a straight st nose and mouth on Face. Sew Face to Head.

With A threaded into needle, whip st over sl sts around Face. Pull sts slightly to soften edge of Face. Draw end of A through to WS of Face.

Sew Arms and Legs to Body. Attach Arms in a vertical position and Legs horizontally, in a seated position. Secure midsection of Legs to Body with a few stitches. Weave in ends. •

Black Cat Door Stopper

Easy

MEASUREMENTS
About 11"/28 cm tall

MATERIALS
YARN
LION BRAND® Vanna's Choice®, 3.5oz/100g balls, each approx 170yd/156m (acrylic/rayon)
- 1 ball each in #153 Black (A), #100 White (B)
- Small amounts of gray and red yarn

HOOK
- One size G-6 (4 mm)

NOTIONS
- Stitch markers
- Tapestry needle
- 2 plastic safety eyes, 9 mm diameter
- Fiberfill stuffing
- Plastic stuffing pellets

GAUGE
Exact gauge is not needed for this project.

NOTE
Work in continuous rnds; do not join or turn unless otherwise instructed.

CAT
HEAD
With A, ch 2.

Rnd 1 Work 6 sc in first ch. Place marker in first st for beg of rnd; move marker up as each rnd is completed.

Rnd 2 Work 2 sc in each st around—12 sts.

Rnd 3 *2 sc in next st, sc in next st, rep from * around—18 sts.

Rnd 4 *2 sc in next st, sc in each of next 2 sts, rep from * around—24 sts.

Rnd 5 *2 sc in next st, sc in each of next 3 sts, rep from * around—30 sts.

Rnd 6 *2 sc in next st, sc in each of next 4 sts, rep from * around—36 sts.

Rnd 7 *2 sc in next st, sc in each of next 5 sts, rep from * around—42 sts.

Rnd 8 *2 sc in next st, sc in each of next 6 sts, rep from * around—48 sts.

Rnds 9-16 Sc in each st around.

Black Cat Door Stopper

Rnd 17 *Sc2tog, sc in each of next 6 sts, rep from * around—42 sts.

Rnd 18 *Sc2tog, sc in each of next 5 sts, rep from * around—36 sts.

Rnd 19 *Sc2tog, sc in each of next 4 sts, rep from * around—30 sts.

Fasten off.

BODY

With B, ch 2.

Rnds 1-8 Work Rnds 1-8 of Head—48 sts.

Rnd 9 *2 sc in next st, sc in each of next 7 sts, rep from * around—54 sts.

Rnd 10 Sc through back loop of each st around.

Rnd 11 *2 sc in next st, sc in each of next 8 sts, rep from * around—60 sts. Change to A.

Rnds 12-30 Sc in each st around.

Rnd 31 *Sc2tog, sc in each of next 8 sts, rep from * around—54 sts.

Rnd 32 Sc in each st around.

Rnd 33 *Sc2tog, sc in each of next 7 sts, rep from * around—48 sts.

Rnd 34 Sc in each st around.

Rnd 35 *Sc2tog, sc in each of next 6 sts, rep from * around—42 sts.

Rnd 36 Sc in each st around.

Rnd 37 *Sc2tog, sc in each of next 5 sts, rep from * around—36 sts.

Rnd 38 Sc in each st around.

Rnd 39 *Sc2tog, sc in each of next 4 sts, rep from * around—30 sts.

Rnds 40-43 Sc in each st around.

Fasten off.

EAR

(Make 2)

With A, ch 2.

Rnd 1 Work 4 sc in first ch. Place marker in first st for beg of rnd; move marker up as each rnd is completed.

Rnd 2 *2 sc in next st, sc in next st, rep from * around—6 sts.

Rnd 3 *2 sc in next st, sc in each of next 2 sts, rep from * around—8 sts.

Rnd 4 *2 sc in next st, sc in each of next 3 sts, rep from * around—10 sts.

Fasten off.

TAIL

Beg at tip of Tail, with B, ch 2.

Rnd 1 Work 4 sc in first ch. Place marker in first st for beg of rnd; move marker up as each rnd is completed.

Rnd 2 Work 2 sc in each st around—8 sts.

Rnds 3-8 Sc2tog, sc in each of next 3 sts, 2 sc in next st, sc in each of next 2 sts—8 sts. Change to A.

Rnds 9-14 Sc2tog, sc in each of next 3 sts, 2 sc in next st, sc in each of next 2 sts—8 sts.

Beg to stuff piece with fiberfill. Continue to stuff as work progresses.

Rnds 15-34 Sc in each st around.

Rnds 35-40 2 sc in next st, sc in each of next 2 sts, sc2tog, sc in each of next 3 sts—8 sts.

Fasten off.

COLLAR

With red yarn, ch 30.

Fasten off.

FINISHING

Following package directions, attach safety eyes to Head. Stuff Head firmly.

With gray yarn, embroider a straight st nose and whiskers. Sew Ears to Head. Stuff Body halfway with pellets, then finish stuffing with fiberfill.

Sew Head to Body. Sew Tail to base of Body and tip of Tail to side of Body. Sew Collar around neck.

Weave in ends. •

Aaron Alien

Easy

MEASUREMENTS
Approx 8"/20.5 cm tall

MATERIALS
YARN
LION BRAND® Feels Like Butta®, 3.5oz/100g balls, each approx 55yd/50m (polyester) [6]
• 1 ball each in #156 Mint (A), #150 Charcoal (B), #100 White (C), #157 Yellow (D)

HOOK
• One size C-2 (2.75 mm)

NOTIONS
• Stitch markers
• Tapestry needle
• Fiberfill stuffing

GAUGE
22 sc = approx 4"/10 cm

Exact gauge is not needed for this project.

NOTES
1) Alien is worked from the top downwards.
2) Two Eye Stalks are worked in continuous rnds and joined together at base of stalks to beg Body. Body is worked in continuous rnds down to Legs. Piece is divided and each Leg worked separately in continuous rnds.
3) Eyes, Mouth, Teeth, and Spots are worked separately and sewn to Alien.
4) Work tightly so that stuffing does not show through spaces between stitches.

ALIEN
FIRST EYE STALK
With A, beg at top of Eye Stalk, ch 2.

Rnd 1 Work 6 sc in second ch from hook. Place marker in first st for beg of rnd; move marker up as each rnd is completed.

Rnd 2 Work 2 sc in each st around—12 sts.

Rnd 3 *Sc in next st, 2 sc in next st; rep from * around—18 sts.

Rnd 4 *Sc in next 2 sts, 2 sc in next st; rep from * around—24 sts.

Aaron Alien

Rnds 5-8 Sc in each st around.
Rnd 9 *Sc in next 2 sts, sc2tog; rep from * around—18 sts.
Rnd 10 *Sc in next st, sc2tog; rep from * around—12 sts.
Rnd 11 *Sc in next 2 sts, sc2tog; rep from * around—9 sts.
Rnds 12-17 Sc in each st around.
Fasten off, stuff firmly.

SECOND EYE STALK

Make same as First Eye Stalk. Stuff firmly but do not fasten off.

BODY

Rnd 1 With A, sc in each st of Second Eye Stalk, ch 6 (for between stalks), sc in each st of last rnd of First Eye Stalk, sc in each ch of ch-6 between stalks—24 sts.
Rnd 2 Sc in next 9 sts, working along opposite side of ch-6 between stalks, sc in next 6 ch, sc in next 15 sts—30 sts.
Rnd 3 Sc in each st around.
Rnd 4 Sc in next 3 sts, 2 sc in next 3 sts, sc in next 12 sts, 2 sc in next 3 sts, sc in next 9 sts—36 sts.
Rnd 5 Sc in next 3 sts, [sc in next st, 2 sc in next st] 3 times, sc in next 12 sts, [sc in next st, 2 sc in next st] 3 times, sc in next 9 sts—42 sts.
Rnd 6 Sc in next 3 sts, [sc in next 2 sts, 2 sc in next st] 3 times, sc in next 12 sts, [sc in next 2 sts, 2 sc in next st] 3 times, sc in next 9 sts—48 sts.
Rnd 7 Sc in each st around.
Rnd 8 Sc in next 3 sts, [sc in next 3 sts, 2 sc in next st] 3 times, sc in next 12 sts, [sc in next 3 sts, 2 sc in next st] 3 times, sc in next 9 sts—54 sts.
Rnd 9 Sc in each st around.
Rnd 10 Sc in next 3 sts, [sc in next 4 sts, 2 sc in next st] 3 times, sc in next 12 sts, [sc in next 4 sts, 2 sc in next st] 3 times, sc in next 9 sts—60 sts.
Rnds 11-19 Sc in each st around.
Rnd 20 Sc in next 3 sts, [sc in next 4 sts, sc2tog] 3 times, sc in next 12 sts, [sc in next 4 sts, sc2tog] 3 times, sc in next 9 sts—54 sts.
Rnd 21 Sc in each st around.
Rnd 22 Sc in next 3 sts, [sc in next 3 sts, sc2tog] 3 times, sc in next 12 sts, [sc in next 3 sts, sc2tog] 3 times, sc in next 9 sts—48 sts.
Rnd 23 Sc in each st around.
Rnd 24 Sc in next 3 sts, [sc in next 2 sts, sc2tog] 3 times, sc in next 12 sts, [sc in next 2 sts, sc2tog] 3 times, sc in next 9 sts—42 sts.
Rnd 25 Sc in each st around.
Stuff body firmly.
Do not fasten off.

FIRST LEG

Rnd 1 Sk 21 sts (for Second Leg), sc in next st, sc in next 20 sts—21 sts.

Rnds 2-8 Sc in each st around.

Rnd 9 *Sc in next st, sc2tog; rep from * around—14 sts.

Fasten off, leaving a long tail for sewing.

Stuff piece firmly.

Thread tail through top of sts of last rnd. Pull tail to close opening at bottom of Leg.

Knot securely.

SECOND LEG

Rnd 1 Join A with sc in first skipped st in Rnd 25 of Body, sc in next 20 sts—21 sts. Place a marker in last sc made to indicate end of rnd; move marker up as each rnd is completed.

Rnds 2-8 Sc in each st around.

Rnd 9 *Sc in next st, sc2tog; rep from * around—14 sts.

Fasten off, leaving a long tail for sewing.

Stuff piece firmly.

Thread tail through top of sts of last rnd. Pull tail to close opening at bottom of Leg.

Knot securely.

EYE

(Make 2)

Pupil

With B, ch 2.

Rnd 1 Work 4 sc in second ch from hook; join with sl st in first sc—4 sts.

Fasten off, leaving a long tail for sewing.

White

With C, ch 4.

Rnd 1 Work 10 dc in fourth ch from hook; join with sl st in first dc—10 sts.

Fasten off, leaving a long tail for sewing. Sew Pupil to White.

With A, embroider a stitch on Pupil for "reflection."

Rep to make second Eye.

MOUTH

With B, ch 11.

Row 1 Sc in second ch from hook and in each ch across—10 sts.

Rows 2-4 Ch 1, turn, sc in each st across.

Row 5 Ch 1, turn, sc2tog, sc in next 6 sts, sc2tog—8 sts.

Row 6 Ch 1, turn, sc in each st across.

Row 7 Ch 1, turn, sc2tog, sc in next 4 sts, sc2tog—6 sts.

Row 8 Ch 1, turn, sc in each st across.

Trim

Rnd 1 Ch 1, turn, sc2tog, sc in next 2 sts, sc2tog; work 8 sc evenly spaced along side edge; working along opposite side of foundation ch, 3 sc in first ch, sc in next 8 ch, 3 sc in next ch; work 8 sc evenly spaced along side edge; join with sl st in first st—34 sts.

Fasten off, leaving a long tail for sewing.

TOOTH

(Make 2)

With C, ch 4.

Row 1 Sc in second ch from hook and in next 2 ch—3 sts.

Rows 2 and 3 Ch 1, turn, sc in each st across.

Row 4 Ch 1, turn, sc2tog, beg in same st as last part of previous sc2tog work another sc2tog—2 sts.

Fasten off, leaving a long tail for sewing.

SMALL SPOT

(Make 2)

With D, ch 2.

Rnd 1 Work 4 sc in second ch from hook; join with sl st in first sc—4 sts.

Fasten off, leaving a long tail for sewing.

LARGE SPOT

With D, ch 4.

Rnd 1 Work 8 dc in fourth ch from hook; join with sl st in first dc—8 sts.

Fasten off, leaving a long tail for sewing.

FINISHING

Using photograph (opposite) as a guide to placement, sew an Eye to top of each Eye Stalk. Sew Teeth to Mouth. Sew Mouth and Spots to Body.

Weave in ends. •

Georgia the Giraffe

Easy

MEASUREMENTS
Approx 15.5"/40.5 cm including horns

MATERIALS
YARN
LION BRAND® Vanna's Choice®, 3.5oz/100g balls, each approx 170yd/156m (acrylic/rayon)
- 1 ball each in #158 Mustard (A), #126 Chocolate (B)
- Small amount of brown yarn

HOOK
- One size H-8 (5 mm)

NOTIONS
- Stitch marker
- Tapestry needle
- 2 plastic safety eyes, 9 mm diameter
- Fiberfill stuffing

GAUGE
Exact gauge is not needed for this project.

NOTE
Work in continuous rnds; do not join or turn unless otherwise instructed.

GIRAFFE
BODY
Beg at top of head, with A, ch 2.

Rnd 1 Work 6 sc in first ch. Place marker in first st for beg of rnd; move marker up as each rnd is completed.

Rnd 2 Work 2 sc in each st around—12 sts.

Rnd 3 *2 sc in next st, sc in next st, rep from * around—18 sts.

Rnd 4 *2 sc in next st, sc in each of next 2 sts, rep from * around—24 sts.

Rnds 5-7 Sc in each st around.

Rnd 8 Work 2 sc in each of first 6 sts, sc in next 18 sts—30 sts.

Rnds 9-11 Sc in each st around.

Rnd 12 (Sc2tog) 6 times, sc in next 18 sts—24 sts.

Rnd 13 *Sc2tog, sc in each of next 2 sts, rep from * around—18 sts.

Following package directions, attach safety eyes to Body. Beg stuffing Body. Continue stuffing firmly as work progresses.

Rnds 14-25 Sc in each st around.

Rnd 26 *2 sc in next st, sc in each of next 5 sts, rep from * around—21 sts.

Rnd 27 *2 sc in next st, sc in each of next 6 sts, rep from * around—24 sts.

Rnd 28 *2 sc in next st, sc in each of next 7 sts, rep from * around—27 sts.

Rnd 29 *2 sc in next st, sc in each of next 8 sts, rep from * around—30 sts.

Rnd 30 *2 sc in next st, sc in each of next 9 sts, rep from * around—33 sts.

Rnd 31 *2 sc in next st, sc in each of next 10 sts, rep from * around—36 sts.

Rnds 32-43 Sc in each st around.

Rnd 44 *Sc2tog, sc in each of next 4 sts, rep from * around—30 sts.

Rnd 45 *Sc2tog, sc in each of next 3 sts, rep from * around—24 sts.

Rnd 46 *Sc2tog, sc in each of next 2 sts, rep from * around—18 sts.

Rnd 47 *Sc2tog, sc in next st, rep from * around—12 sts.

Rnd 48 (Sc2tog) around—6 sts.

Fasten off.

LEG

(Make 4)

With B, ch 2.

Rnd 1 Work 6 sc in first ch. Place marker in first st for beg of rnd; move marker up as each rnd is completed.

Rnd 2 Work 2 sc in each st around—12 sts.

Rnd 3 *2 sc in next st, sc in next st, rep from * around—18 sts.

Rnd 4 *Working through back loops only*, sc in each st around.

Rnd 5 *Sc2tog, sc in next st, rep from * around—12 sts. Change to A.

Rnds 6-22 Sc in each st around.

Fasten off.

HORN

(Make 2)

With B, ch 2.

Rnd 1 Work 4 sc in first ch. Place marker in first st for beg of rnd; move marker up as each rnd is completed.

Rnd 2 Work 2 sc in each st around—8 sts.

Rnd 3 Sc in each st around.

Rnd 4 (Sc2tog) around—4 sts.

Stuff firmly. Change to A.

Rnds 5-7 Sc in each st around.

Fasten off.

EAR

(Make 2)

With B, ch 2.

Rnd 1 Work 6 sc in first ch. Place marker in first st for beg of rnd; move marker up as each rnd is completed.

Rnd 2 Work 2 sc in each st around—12 sts.

Fasten off.

TAIL

With A, ch 15. Change to B.

Ch 5, sl st to last A ch, ch 5, sl st to same last A ch, ch 5, sl st, and end at same ch.

Fasten off.

SMALL SPOT

(Make 3)

With B, ch 2.

Work Rnd 1 of Ear.

Fasten off.

LARGE SPOT

(Make 2)

Work as for Ear.

FINISHING

Sew Horns to top of Body. Fold Ears and sew to Body. Stuff Arms and Legs lightly and sew to Body. Sew Tail to back of Body. Sew Spots as desired onto Body. With brown yarn, embroider straight st nose and mouth. Weave in ends. •

Olivia Octopus

Easy

MEASUREMENTS
Approx 3"/7.5 cm tall

MATERIALS
YARN
LION BRAND® Vanna's Choice®, 3.5oz/100g balls, each approx 170yd/156m (acrylic/rayon) (4)
- 1 ball in #145 Eggplant
- Small amount of red yarn

HOOK
- One size G-6 (4 mm)

NOTIONS
- Stitch marker
- Tapestry needle
- 2 plastic safety eyes, 9 mm diameter
- Fiberfill stuffing

GAUGE
Exact gauge is not needed for this project.

NOTE
Work in continuous rnds; do not join or turn unless otherwise instructed.

OCTOPUS
BODY
Ch 2.

Rnd 1 Work 6 sc in first ch. Place marker in first st for beg of rnd; move marker up as each rnd is completed.

Rnd 2 2 sc in each st around—12 sts.

Rnd 3 *2 sc in next st, sc in next st; rep from * around—18 sts.

Rnd 4 *2 sc in next st, sc in each of next 2 sts; rep from * around—24 sts.

Rnd 5 *2 sc in next st, sc in each of next 3 sts; rep from * around—30 sts.

Rnd 6 *2 sc in next st, sc in each of next 4 sts; rep from * around—36 sts.

Rnd 7 *2 sc in next st, sc in each of next 5 sts; rep from * around—42 sts.

Rnds 8-17 Sc in each st around.

Rnd 18 *Sc2tog, sc in each of next 5 sts; rep from * around—36 sts.

Rnd 19 *Sc2tog, sc in each of next 4 sts; rep from * around—30 sts.

Rnd 20 *Sc2tog, sc in each of next 3 sts; rep from * around—24 sts.

Following package directions, attach safety eyes. Stuff piece.

Rnd 21 *Sc2tog, sc in next 2 sts; rep from * around—18 sts.

Rnd 22 *Sc2tog, sc in next st; rep from * around—12 sts.

Rnd 23 (Sc2tog) around—6 sts.

Fasten off, leaving a long tail. Weave tail through last rnd and gather tightly. Knot to secure.

TENTACLE
(Make 8)

Ch 2.

Rnd 1 Work 6 sc in first ch. Place marker to indicate beg of rnd; move marker up as each rnd is completed.

Rnd 2 2 sc in each sc around—12 sts.

Rnds 3-10 Sc in each sc around.

Fasten off.

FINISHING
Stuff Tentacles and sew to Body.

With red yarn, embroider straight st smile.

Weave in ends. •

Genie the Ghost

Easy

MEASUREMENTS
Approx 4"/10 cm tall

MATERIALS
YARN
LION BRAND® Vanna's Choice®, 3.5oz/100g balls, each approx 170yd/156m (acrylic/rayon) (4)
- 1 ball in #100 White
- Small amount black yarn

HOOK
- One size G-6 (4 mm)

NOTIONS
- Stitch marker
- Tapestry needle
- 2 plastic safety eyes, 6 mm diameter
- Fiberfill stuffing

GAUGE
Exact gauge is not needed for this project.

NOTE
Work in continuous rnds; do not join or turn unless otherwise instructed.

GHOST
HEAD AND BODY
Ch 2.

Rnd 1 Work 3 sc in first ch. Place marker in first st for beg of rnd; move marker up as each rnd is completed.

Rnd 2 Sc in each st around.

Rnd 3 Work 2 sc in each st around—6 sts.

Rnd 4 Sc in each st around.

Rnd 5 *2 sc in next st, rep from * around 3 times, sc in each of last 3 sts—9 sts.

Rnd 6 *2 sc in next st, sc in next st, rep from * around 3 times, sc in each of last 3 sts—12 sts.

Rnd 7 *2 sc in next st, sc in each of next 2 sts, rep from * around 3 times, sc in each of last 3 sts—15 sts.

Rnd 8 *2 sc in next st, sc in each of next 3 sts, rep from * around 3 times, sc in each of last 3 sts—18 sts.

Rnd 9 *2 sc in next st, sc in each of next 4 sts, rep from * around 3 times, sc in each of last 3 sts—21 sts.

Rnd 10 *2 sc in next st, sc in each of next 5 sts, rep from * around 3 times, sc in each of last 3 sts—24 sts.

Rnds 11 and 12 Sc in each st around.

Following package instructions, attach safety eyes.

Rnd 13 *Sc2tog, sc in each of next 2 sts, rep from * around—18 sts.

Rnd 14 *2 sc in next st, sc in each of next 2 sts, rep from * around—24 sts.

Rnd 15 *2 sc in next st, sc in each of next 3 sts, rep from * around—30 sts.

Rnds 16-19 Sc in each st around.

Rnd 20 *Sc2tog, sc in each of next 3 sts, rep from * around—24 sts.

Begin stuffing; add more stuffing as work progresses.

Rnd 21 *Sc2tog, sc in each of next 2 sts, rep from * around—18 sts.

Rnd 22 *Sc2tog, sc in next st, rep from * around—12 sts.

Rnd 23 *Sc2tog, rep from * around—6 sts.

Fasten off.

ARM
(Make 2)

Ch 2.

Rnd 1 Work 6 sc in first ch. Place marker in first st for beg of rnd; move marker up as each rnd is completed.

Rnds 2-5 Sc in each st around.

Fasten off.

FINISHING

With black yarn, embroider a straight st smile.

Lightly stuff Arms and sew to sides of Body.

Weave in ends. •

Leo the Lion

Easy

MEASUREMENTS
Approx 11"/28 cm tall

MATERIALS
YARN
LION BRAND® Wool-Ease®, 3oz/85g balls, each approx 197yd/180m (acrylic/wool) [4]
- 2 balls in #122 Sienna (A)
- 1 ball in #126 Chocolate Brown (small amount) (B)

LION BRAND® Fun Fur®, 1.75oz/50g balls, each approx 64yd/58m (polyester) [5]
- 1 ball in #126 Chocolate 1 ball (C)

HOOK
- One size H-8 (5 mm)

NOTIONS
- Stitch marker
- Tapestry needle
- Fiberfill stuffing

GAUGE
17 sc and 17 rows = 4"/10 cm with A.
Exact gauge is not needed for this project.

NOTE
Work in continuous rnds; do not join or turn unless otherwise instructed.

LION
HEAD
With A, ch 6.

Foundation rnd Sl st in third ch from hook and next 3 ch, ch 2. Do not turn, working in free loops on opposite side of beg ch, sc in first 4 ch, 3 sc in beg ch-2 sp; pivot to work in sl sts at beg of rnd, sc in each of 4 sl sts, 3 sc in end ch-2 sp; do not join—14 sts. Place marker to indicate beg of rnd; move marker up as each rnd is completed.

Rnd 1 Sc in next 4 sc, 2 sc in next sc, sc in next sc, 2 sc in next sc, sc in next 4 sc, 2 sc in next sc, sc in next sc, 2 sc in next sc—18 sts.

Rnd 2 Sc in next 3 sc, 2 sc in next sc, sc in next 3 sc, 2 sc in next sc, sc in next 4 sc, 2 sc in next sc, sc in next 3 sc, 2 sc in next sc, sc in next sc—22 sts.

Rnd 3 Sc in next 4 sc, 2 sc in next sc, sc in next 3 sc, 2 sc in next sc, sc in next 6 sc, 2 sc in next sc, sc in next 3 sc, 2 sc in next sc, sc in next 2 sc—26 sts.

Rnds 4 and 5 Sc in each sc around.

Rnd 6 (Sc in next 8 sc, sc2tog, sc in next sc, sc2tog) twice—22 sts.

Rnds 7 and 8 Sc in each sc around.

Rnd 9 2 sc in next sc, sc in next sc, 2 sc in next sc, sc in next 6 sc, (2 sc in next sc, sc in next sc) twice, 2 sc in next sc, sc in next 6 sc, 2 sc in next sc, sc in next sc—28 sts.

Rnds 10-12 Sc in each sc around.

Rnd 13 Sc in next sc, 2 sc in next sc, sc in next 11 sc, 2 sc in next sc, sc in next sc, 2 sc in next sc, sc in next 11 sc, 2 sc in next sc—32 sts.

Rnds 14-17 Sc in each sc around.

Rnd 18 (Sc in next 2 sc, sc2tog) 8 times—24 sts. Stuff Head with fiberfill.

Rnd 19 (Sc in next sc, sc2tog) 8 times—16 sts.

Rnd 20 (Sc2tog) 8 times—8 sts.

Rnd 21 Sc in each sc around.

Sl st in next sc.

Fasten off, leaving a long tail. Weave tail through last rnd, gather tightly and fasten off.

BODY
Note Work begins at neck.

With A, ch 3; join with sl st in first ch to form a ring.

Leo the Lion

Rnd 1 Work 6 sc in ring; do not join. Place marker to indicate beg of rnd; move marker up as each rnd is completed.

Rnd 2 Work 2 sc in each sc around—12 sts.

Rnd 3 Sc in each sc around.

Rnd 4 (Sc in next sc, 2 sc in next sc) around—18 sts.

Rnd 5 (Sc in next 2 sc, 2 sc in next sc) around—24 sts.

Rnd 6 Sc in each sc around.

Rnd 7 (Sc in next 3 sc, 2 sc in next sc) around—30 sts.

Rnd 8 (Sc in next 4 sc, 2 sc in next sc) around—36 sts.

Rnd 9 Sc in each sc around.

Rep Rnd 9 until Body measures 8"/20.5 cm.

Next rnd (Sc in next sc, sc2tog) 12 times—24 sts. Stuff Body.

Next rnd (Sc in next sc, sc2tog) 8 times—16 sts.

Next rnd (Sc in next 2 sc, sc2tog) 4 times—12 sts.

Last rnd (Sc in next 2 sc, sc2tog) 3 times—9 sts.

Sl st in next sc.

Fasten off, leaving a long tail. Weave tail through last rnd, gather tightly and fasten off.

BACK LEG

(Make 2)

With A, ch 3; join with sl st in first ch to form a ring.

Rnd 1 Work 6 sc in ring; do not join. Place marker to indicate beg of rnd; move marker as each rnd is completed.

Rnd 2 Work 2 sc in each sc around—12 sts.

Rnd 3 (Sc in next sc, 2 sc in next sc) around—18 sts.

Rnds 4 and 5 Sc in each sc around.

Rnd 6 (Sc in next sc, sc2tog) around—12 sts.

Rnds 7-13 Sc in each sc around.

Note Change to working back and forth in rows.

Row 14 Ch 1, turn sc in first 6 sc; leave rem sts unworked.

Row 15 Ch 1, turn, sc in first 4 sc; leave last 2 sc unworked.

Row 16 Ch 1, turn, sc in first 2 sc; leave last 2 sc unworked.

Row 17 Ch 1, turn, sc in first 2 sc, sc in unworked sc in row below; leave 1 sc unworked—3 sts.

Row 18 Ch 1, turn, sc in first 3 sc, sc in unworked sc in row below; leave 1 sc unworked—4 sts.

Row 19 Ch 1, turn, sc in first 4 sc, sc in unworked sc in row below—5 sts.

Row 20 Ch 1, turn, sc in first 5 sc, sc in unworked sc in row below—6 sts.

Rnd 21 Ch 1, turn, sc in first 6 sc; insert hook in edge of work and draw up a loop, insert hook in unworked sc in row below and draw up a loop, yarn over, and draw through all loops on hook (edge-sc2tog made); sc in next 4 sc; insert hook in next sc and draw up a loop, insert hook in edge of work and draw up a loop, yarn over, and draw through all loops on hook (edge-sc2tog made); do not join—12 sts.

Note Change to working in rnds.

Rnds 22 and 23 Sc in each sc around.

Rnd 24 (Sc in next sc, 2 sc in next sc) around—18 sts.

Rnd 25 Sc in each sc around.

Rnd 26 (Sc in next 2 sc, 2 sc in next sc) around—24 sts.

Rnd 27 Sc in each sc around.

Rnd 28 (Sc in next 3 sc, 2 sc in next sc) around—30 sts.

Rnd 29 Sc in each sc around.

Rnd 30 (Sc in next 9 sc, 2 sc in next sc) 3 times—33 sts.

Rnds 31 and 32 Sc in each sc around.

Rnd 33 (Sc in next 9 sc, sc2tog) 3 times—30 sts.

Rnd 34 (Sc in next 3 sc, sc2tog) around—24 sts. Stuff Leg.

Rnd 35 (Sc in next 2 sc, sc2tog) around—18 sts.

Rnd 36 (Sc in next sc, sc2tog) around—12 sts.

Rnd 37 (Sc2tog) 6 times—6 sts.

Sl st in next sc.

Fasten off, leaving a long tail. Weave tail through last rnd, gather tightly and fasten off.

FRONT LEG

(Make 2)

Rnds 1-6 Work Rnds 1-6 as for Back Leg.

Rnd 7 Sc in each sc around.

Rep Rnd 7 until Leg measures 7"/18 cm.

Fasten off.

EAR

(Make 2)

With A, ch 3; join with sl st in first ch to form a ring.

Rnd 1 Work 6 sc in ring; do not join. Place marker to indicate beg of rnd; move marker as each rnd is completed.

Rnd 2 2 sc in each sc around—12 sts.

Rnds 3 and 4 Sc in each sc around.

Sl st in next sc.

Fasten off, leaving a long tail for sewing. Flatten Ear.

TAIL

With A, ch 3; join with sl st in first ch to form a ring.

Rnd 1 Work 6 sc in ring; do not join.

Rnd 2 Sc in each sc around

Rep Rnd 2 until Tail measures 7"/18 cm.

Fasten off.

FINISHING

Sew Head to Body.

MANE

With 2 strands of C held together, and leaving a 3"/7.5 cm yarn tail, work surface sl sts around back of Head and top of back of Body, as follows:

1) Insert hook into Lion around a st.

2) Yarn over with C.

3) Draw loop of C back through st of Lion.

4) Insert hook around next st of Lion.

Rep from step 2, working Mane randomly around Head and shoulders of Lion.

To finish, cut C leaving a 3"/7.5 cm tail. Draw tail through last loop of C. Draw tails of C into Lion to hide.

TAIL TUFT

Work as for Mane around tip of Tail. Weave yarn ends through beg ring.

ASSEMBLY

Stuff Front Legs and sew to Body. Sew Back Legs to Body. Sew Ears to Head. Sew Tail to lower back of Body.

With B, embroider straight st whiskers, claws, and features.

Weave in ends. •

Bryan Bookworm

Easy

MEASUREMENTS
Approx 4.25"/11 cm long

MATERIALS
YARN
LION BRAND® Wool-Ease®, 3oz/85g balls, each approx 197yd/180m (acrylic/wool) (4)
- 1 ball each in #174 Avocado (A), #153 Black (B)
- Small amounts of brown, red, and yellow yarn

HOOK
- One size G-6 (4 mm)

NOTIONS
- Stitch marker
- Tapestry needle
- 2 small black beads (for eyes)
- Fiberfill stuffing

GAUGE
Exact gauge is not needed for this project.

NOTE
Work in continuous rnds; do not join rnds or turn unless otherwise instructed.

WORM
HEAD AND BODY
With A, ch 2.

Rnd 1 Work 6 sc in first ch. Place marker in first st for beg of rnd; move marker up as each rnd is completed.

Rnd 2 2 sc in each st around—12 sts.

Rnd 3 *2 sc in next st, sc in next st; rep from * around—18 sts.

Rnd 4 *2 sc in next st, sc in next 2 sts; rep from * around—24 sts.

Rnds 5-8 Sc in each st around.

Rnd 9 *Sc2tog, sc in next 2 sts; rep from * around—18 sts.

Rnd 10 *Sc2tog, sc in next st; rep from * around—12 sts. Start stuffing firmly. Continue stuffing as you go.

Rnd 11 (Sc2tog) 6 times—6 sts.

Rnd 12 2 sc in each st around—12 sts.

Rnd 13 Rep Rnd 3—18 sts.

Rnds 14-17 Sc in each st around.

Rnd 18 Rep Rnd 10—12 sts.

Rnd 19 Rep Rnd 11—6 sts.

Rnd 20 Rep Rnd 12—12 sts.

Rnds 21-23 Sc in each st around.

Rnd 24 *Sc2tog, sc in next 2 sts; rep from * around—9 sts.

Rnd 25 Rep Rnd 18—6 sts.

Rnd 26 (Sc2tog) 3 times—3 sts.
Fasten off.

CAP
With B, ch 2.

Rnds 1 and 2 Work Rnds 1 and 2 of Head and Body—12 sts.

Rnds 3 and 4 Sc in each st around.
Fasten off.

MORTARBOARD
With B, ch 7.

Row 1 Sc in second ch from hook and in each ch across—6 sts.

Rows 2-7 Ch 1, turn, sc in each st across.
Fasten off.

FINISHING

Sew beads to Head for eyes. With brown yarn, embroider outline st eyeglasses around beads. With red yarn, embroider straight st smile.

Sew Mortarboard to Cap, then sew Cap to Head. Sew strand of yellow yarn to center top of Mortarboard for tassel, fray end of strand. Weave in ends. •

Paula Puppy

Easy

MEASUREMENTS
Approx 12"/30.5 cm tall

MATERIALS
YARN
LION BRAND® Vanna's Choice®, 3.5oz/100g balls, each approx 170yd/156m (acrylic/rayon) 〔4〕
- 1 ball each in #126 Chocolate (A), #140 Dusty Rose (B), #123 Beige (C), #173 Dusty Green (D)
- Small amount of black yarn

HOOK
- One size H-8 (5 mm)

NOTIONS
- Stitch marker
- Tapestry needle
- 2 plastic safety eyes, 9 mm diameter
- Fiberfill stuffing

GAUGE
Exact gauge is not needed for this project.

NOTE
Work in continuous rnds; do not join or turn unless otherwise instructed.

PUPPY
HEAD AND BODY
Beg at top of Head, with A, ch 2.

Rnd 1 Work 6 sc in first ch. Place marker in first st for beg of rnd; move marker up as each rnd is completed.

Rnd 2 Work 2 sc in each st around—12 sts.

Rnd 3 *2 sc in next st, sc in next st, rep from * around—18 sts.

Rnd 4 *2 sc in next st, sc in each of next 2 sts, rep from * around—24 sts.

Rnd 5 *2 sc in next st, sc in each of next 3 sts, rep from * around—30 sts.

Rnd 6 *2 sc in next st, sc in each of next 4 sts, rep from * around—36 sts.

Rnd 7 *2 sc in next st, sc in each of next 5 sts, rep from * around—42 sts.

Rnds 8-12 Sc in each st around.

Rnd 13 2 sc in each of first 6 sts, sc in rem sts around—48 sts.

Rnds 14-17 Sc in each st around.

Rnd 18 *Sc2tog, sc in each of next 6 sts, rep from * around—42 sts.

Rnd 19 *Sc2tog, sc in each of next 5 sts, rep from * around—36 sts.

Rnd 20 *Sc2tog, sc in each of next 4 sts, rep from * around—30 sts.

Rnd 21 *Sc2tog, sc in each of next 3 sts, rep from * around—24 sts. Change to B.

Rnd 22 Sc in each st around.

Following package directions, attach safety eyes to Head. Begin stuffing Body. Continue stuffing piece firmly as work progresses.

Rnd 23 *2 sc in next st, sc in each of next 3 sts, rep from * around—30 sts.

Rnd 24 *2 sc in next st, sc in each of next 4 sts, rep from * around—36 sts. Change to C.

Rnd 25 Sc in each st around. Change to D.

Rnds 26 and 27 Sc in each st around. Change to B.

Rnds 28-30 Sc in each st around. Change to C.

Rnd 31 Sc in each st around. Change to D.

Rnds 32 and 33 Sc in each st around. Change to B.

Rnds 34-36 Sc in each st around. Change to A.

Rnds 37-39 Sc in each st around.

Paula Puppy

Rnd 40 *Sc2tog, sc in each of next 4 sts, rep from * around—30 sts.

Rnd 41 *Sc2tog, sc in each of next 3 sts, rep from * around—24 sts.

Rnd 42 *Sc2tog, sc in each of next 2 sts, rep from * around—18 sts.

Rnd 43 *Sc2tog, sc in next st, rep from * around—12 sts.

Rnd 44 (Sc2tog) around—6 sts.

Fasten off.

ARM

(Make 2)

With A, ch 2.

Rnd 1 Work 6 sc in first ch. Place marker in first st for beg of rnd; move marker up as each rnd is completed.

Rnd 2 Work 2 sc in each st around—12 sts.

Rnds 3-5 Sc in each st around. Change to B.

Rnds 6-8 Sc in each st around. Change to D.

Rnds 9 and 10 Sc in each st around. Change to C.

Rnd 11 Sc in each st around. Change to B.

Rnds 12-14 Sc in each st around.

Fasten off.

LEG

(Make 2)

With A, ch 2.

Rnd 1 Work 6 sc in first ch. Place marker in first st for beg of rnd; move marker up as each rnd is completed.

Rnd 2 Work 2 sc in each st around—12 sts.

Rnds 3-17 Sc in each st around.

Fasten off.

EAR

(Make 2)

With A, ch 2.

Rnd 1 Work 6 sc in first ch. Place marker in first st for beg of rnd; move marker up as each rnd is completed.

Rnd 2 Work 2 sc in each st around—12 sts.

Rnd 3 *2 sc in next st, sc in next st, rep from * around—18 sts.

Rnds 4-7 Sc in each st around.

Rnd 8 *Sc2tog, sc in each of next 5 sts, sc2tog, rep from * around—14 sts.

Rnd 9 Sc in each st around.

Rnd 10 *Sc2tog, sc in each of next 3 sts, sc2tog, rep from * around—10 sts.

Rnd 11 Sc in each st around.

Rnd 12 *Sc2tog, sc in next st, sc2tog, rep from * around—6 sts.

Rnd 13 Sc in each st around.

Fasten off.

TAIL

With A, ch 2.

Rnd 1 Work 4 sc in first ch. Place marker in first st for beg of rnd; move marker up as each rnd is completed.

Rnd 2 Sc in each st around—4 sts.

Rnd 3 *2 sc in next st, sc in next st, rep from * around—6 sts.

Rnd 4 Sc in each st around.

Rnd 5 *2 sc in next st, sc in each of next 2 sts, rep from * around—8 sts.

Rnd 6 Sc in each st around.

Rnds 7-11 Sc2tog, sc in next st, 2 sc in each of next 2 sts, sc in next st, sc2tog.

Fasten off.

FINISHING

Sew Ears to Body. Stuff Arms and Legs lightly and sew to Body. Sew Tail to back of Body.

With black yarn, embroider straight st nose.

Weave in ends. •

Mini Frog, Parrot, and Duck

Easy

MEASUREMENTS
Frog: approx 3½"/9 cm tall
Parrot: approx 3½"/9 cm tall
Duck: approx 4"/10 cm tall

MATERIALS
YARN
LION BRAND® Bonbons®, 0.35oz/10g balls, each approx 3.5yd/3.25m (acrylic) (3)
- 1 pack #610 Brights: Green (A), Pink (B), Magenta (C), Blue (D), Purple (E), Orange (F), Yellow (G), Coral (H)

LION BRAND® Jamie®, 1.75oz/50g balls, each approx 137yd/125m (acrylic) (3)
- 1 ball in #100 Angel White (I)
- Small amount of black yarn

HOOK
- One size F-5 (3.75 mm)

NOTIONS
- Stitch markers
- Tapestry needle
- Fiberfill stuffing

GAUGE
Exact gauge is not needed for this project.

NOTES
1) Work in continuous rnds; do not join or turn unless otherwise instructed.
2) To change color, work last st of old color to last yarn over. Yarn over with new color and draw through all loops to complete st. Fasten off old color.

FROG
BODY
With A, ch 2.
Rnd 1 Work 6 sc in first ch. Place marker in first st for beg of rnd; move marker up as each rnd is completed.
Rnd 2 2 sc in each sc around—12 sc.
Rnd 3 *2 sc in next sc, sc in next sc; rep from * around—18 sc.
Rnd 4 *2 sc in next sc, sc in next 2 sc; rep from * around—24 sc.
Rnd 5 *2 sc in next sc, sc in next 3 sc; rep from * around—30 sc.
Rnds 6-12 Sc in each sc around.

Mini Frog, Parrot, and Duck

Rnd 13 *Sc2tog, sc in next 3 sc; rep from * around—24 sc.

Rnd 14 *Sc2tog, sc in next 2 sc; rep from * around—18 sc.

Rnd 15 *Sc2tog, sc in next sc; rep from * around—12 sc.

Stuff piece.

Rnd 16 (Sc2tog) around—6 sc.

Fasten off, leaving a long yarn tail. Weave tail through last rnd and gather tightly. Knot to secure.

EYE

(Make 2)

With I, ch 2.

Rnd 1 Work 6 sc in first ch. Place marker in first st for beg of rnd; move marker up as each rnd is completed.

Rnd 2 Work 2 sc in each sc around—12 sc.

Rnds 3 and 4 Sc in each sc around.

Fasten off.

FINISHING

Join A to Body with sl st, ch 10.

Work (sl st, ch 5, sl st, ch 3, sl st) in fourth ch from hook. Fasten off. Rep to make a total of 4 legs.

With black yarn, embroider straight st pupils on each Eye. With B, embroider straight st smile onto Body. Stuff Eyes lightly and sew to Body.

Weave in ends.

PARROT

BODY

With C, work as for Frog Body (page 45).

EYE

(Make 2)

With I, ch 2.

Rnd 1 Work 6 sc in first ch.

Rnd 2 Work 2 sc in each st around—12 sts.

Fasten off.

WING

(Make 2)

With D, ch 2.

Rnd 1 Work 6 sc in first ch. Place marker in first st for beg of rnd; move marker up as each rnd is completed.

Rnd 2 Work 2 sc in each st around—12 sts.

Rnds 3-5 Sc in each st around.

Change to E.

Rnds 6 and 7 With E, sc in each st around.

Change to C.

Rnds 8 and 9 With C, sc in each st around.

Rnd 10 (Sc2tog) around—6 sts.

Fasten off.

FOOT

(Make 2)

With F, ch 2.

Rnd 1 Work 8 sc in first ch. Place marker in first st for beg of rnd; move marker up as each rnd is completed.

Rnd 2 Sc in each st around—8 sts.

Rnd 3 (Sc2tog) around—4 sts.

Fasten off.

BEAK

With F, ch 2.

Rnd 1 Work 4 sc in first ch. Place marker in first st for beg of rnd; move marker up as each rnd is completed.

Rnd 2 Sc in first st, work 2 sc in each of next 2 sts, sc in last st—6 sts.

Rnd 3 Sc in each of first 2 sts, work 2 sc in each of next 2 sts, sc in each of last 2 sts—8 sts.

Rnd 4 Sc in each of first 3 sts, work 2 sc in each of next 2 sts, sc in each of last 3 sts—10 sts.

Rnd 5 Sc in each of first 4 sts, work 2 sc in each of next 2 sts, sc in each of last 4 sts—12 sts.

Rnd 6 Sc each of first 5 sts, work 2 sc in each of the next 2 sts, sc in each of last 5 sts—14 sts.

Fasten off.

FINISHING

Stuff Beak and sew to Body. With black yarn, embroider straight st pupils on each Eye and sew to Body. Lightly stuff Wings and Feet and sew to Body.

Weave in ends.

DUCK

BODY

Beg at top of head, with G, ch 2.

Rnd 1 Work 6 sc in first ch. Place marker in first st for beg of rnd; move marker up as each rnd is completed.

Rnd 2 Work 2 sc in each sc around—12 sts.

Rnd 3 *2 sc in next st, sc in next st, rep from * around—18 sts.

Rnd 4 *2 sc in next st, sc in each of next 2 sts, rep from * around—24 sts.

Rnd 5 *2 sc in next st, sc in each of next 3 sts, rep from * around—30 sts.

Rnd 6 *2 sc in next st, sc in each of next 4 sts, rep from * around—36 sts.

Rnds 7-18 Sc in each st around.

Fasten off.

WING

(Make 2)

With F, ch 2.

Rnd 1 Work 6 sc in first ch. Place marker in first st for beg of rnd; move marker up as each rnd is completed.

Rnd 2 Work 2 sc in each st around—12 sts.

Rnds 3-7 Sc in each st around.

Rnd 8 *Sc2tog, sc in each of next 2 sts, rep from * to last 2 sts, sc2tog—8 sts.

Fasten off.

FOOT

(Make 2)

With H, ch 2.

Rnd 1 Work 8 sc in first ch. Place marker in first st for beg of rnd; move marker up as each rnd is completed.

Rnd 2 Work 2 sc in each st around—16 sc.

Rnd 3 Sc in each st around.

Rnd 4 *Sc2tog, sc in each of next 4 sts, rep from * to last 2 sts, sc2tog—12 sts.

Fasten off.

BEAK

With H, ch 2.

Rnd 1 Work 6 sc in first ch. Place marker in first st for beg of rnd; move marker up as each rnd is completed.

Rnd 2 Work 2 sc in each st around—12 sts.

Rnd 3 *2 sc in next st, sc in next st, rep from * around—18 sts.

Rnd 4 *2 sc in next st, sc in each of next 2 sts, rep from * around—24 sts.

Fasten off.

FINISHING

Lightly stuff Wings and Feet and sew to Body. Fold Beak in half to form semicircle. Stitch rounded edges together and sew straight edge to Body. With black yarn, embroider straight st eyes onto Body. Stuff Body and sew closed. Weave in ends. •

Bunny Bride and Groom

Easy

MEASUREMENTS
Approx 6"/15 cm x 6"/15 cm

MATERIALS
YARN
LION BRAND® Vanna's Choice®, 3.5oz/100g balls, each approx 170yd/156m (acrylic/rayon)
- 1 ball each in #099 Linen (A), #153 Black (B), #100 White (C)
- Small amount of pink yarn

HOOK
One size G-6 (4 mm)

NOTIONS
- Stitch marker
- Tapestry needle
- 4 safety eyes, 6 mm
- Fiberfill stuffing

GAUGE
Exact gauge is not needed for this project.

NOTES
1) Work in continuous rnds; do not join rnds or turn unless otherwise instructed.
2) To change color, work last st of old color to last yarn over; yarn over with new color, and draw through all loops on hook to complete st.

BUNNY BRIDE AND GROOM
HEAD
(Make 2)
With A, ch 2.

Rnd 1 Work 6 sc in second ch from hook. Place marker for beg of rnd; move marker up as each rnd is completed.

Rnd 2 2 sc in each st around—12 sts.

Rnd 3 *2 sc in next st, sc in next st; rep from * around—18 sts.

Rnd 4 *2 sc in next st, sc in next 2 sts; rep from * around—24 sts.

Rnds 5-10 Sc in each st around.

Rnd 11 *Sc2tog, sc in next 2 sts; rep from * around—18 sts.

Rnd 12 *Sc2tog, sc in next st; rep from * around—12 sts.
Fasten off.

BODY
(Make 1 with B and 1 with C)
Ch 2.

Rnds 1-4 Work Rnds 1-4 of Head—24 sts.

Rnds 5-11 Sc in each st around.

Rnds 12 and 13 Work Rnds 11 and 12 of Head—12 sts.
Fasten off.

ARM
Groom
(Make 2)
With A, ch 2.

Rnd 1 Work 6 sc in second ch from hook. Place marker for beg of rnd; move marker up as each rnd is completed.

Rnd 2 Sc in each st around; change to B in last st.

Rnds 3-5 Sc in each st around.
Fasten off.

Bride
(Make 2)
With A, ch 2.

Rnd 1 Work 6 sc in second ch from hook. Place marker for beg of rnd; move marker up as each rnd is completed.

Rnds 2-5 Sc in each st around.
Fasten off.

EAR

(Make 4)

With A, ch 2.

Rnd 1 Work 4 sc in second ch from hook. Place marker for beg of rnd; move marker up as each rnd is completed.

Rnd 2 Sc in each st around.

Rnd 3 *2 sc in next st, sc in next st; rep from * once more—6 sts.

Rnd 4 Sc in each st around.

Rnd 5 *2 sc in next st, sc in next 2 sts; rep from * once more—8 sts.

Rnds 6-9 Sc in each st around.

Fasten off.

GROOM'S VEST

With C, ch 5.

Row 1 Sc in second ch from hook and in each ch across—4 sts.

Rows 2-4 Ch 1, turn, sc in each st across.

Row 5 Ch 1, turn, (sc2tog) twice—2 sts.

Row 6 Ch 1, turn, sc2tog—1 st.

Fasten off.

Bunny Bride and Groom

BRIDE'S SKIRT

With C, ch 25.

Row 1 Sc in second ch from hook and in each ch across—24 sts.

Row 2 Ch 1, turn, 2 sc in each st across—48 sts.

Row 3 Ch 1, turn, sc in each st across.

Row 4 (ruffle) Ch 1, turn, *(sc, hdc) in next st, dc in next st, (hdc, sc) in next st, sl st in next st; rep from * across. Fasten off.

VEIL

With C, ch 4.

Row 1 Sc in second ch from hook and in each ch across—3 sts.

Row 2 Ch 1, turn, sc in each st across.

Row 3 Ch 2, turn, 3 hdc in each st across—9 sts.

Row 4 Ch 2, turn, 2 hdc in each st across—18 sts.

Rows 5-7 Ch 2, turn, hdc in each st across.

Row 8 (ruffle) Ch 1, turn, *(sc, hdc) in next st, (hdc, sc) in next st, sl st in next st; rep from * across. Fasten off.

FLOWER

(Make 4; 3 for Bride's Veil, 1 for Groom)

With small amount of pink yarn, ch 2.

Rnd 1 (Hdc, sl st) 6 times in second ch from hook. Fasten off.

BASE

With C, ch 2.

Rnd 1 Work 6 sc in second ch from hook. Place marker for beg of rnd; move marker up as each rnd is completed.

Rnd 2 2 sc in each st around—12 sts.

Rnd 3 *2 sc in next st, sc in next st; rep from * around—18 sts.

Rnd 4 *2 sc in next st, sc in next 2 sts; rep from * around—24 sts.

Rnd 5 *2 sc in next st, sc in next 3 sts; rep from * around—30 sts.

Rnd 6 *2 sc in next st, sc in next 4 sts; rep from * around—36 sts.

Rnd 7 *2 sc in next st, sc in next 5 sts; rep from * around—42 sts.

Rnd 8 *2 sc in next st, sc in next 6 sts; rep from * around—48 sts.

Rnd 9 *2 sc in next st, sc in next 7 sts; rep from * around—54 sts.

Rnd 10 *2 sc in next st, sc in next 8 sts; rep from * around—60 sts.

Rnd 11 (ruffle) *(Sc, hdc) in next st, dc in next st, (hdc, sc) in next st, sl st in next st; rep from * around. Fasten off.

FINISHING

Following package directions, attach safety eyes to faces. Firmly stuff each Head and sew one to each Body. Sew 2 Ears to top of each Head.

Stuff Arms lightly and sew B colored Arms to B colored Body, and A colored Arms to C colored Body.

With a scrap of pink yarn, embroider a nose on each face.

Groom

Arrange Vest piece on center of chest and sew in place. Tie a short length of B around neck for tie and embroider French knots for buttons. Sew one Flower onto chest.

Bride

Arrange Skirt around Body and sew in place. Sew Veil on top of Head. Sew 3 Flowers on top of Veil.

Bride and Groom

Sew Bride and Groom to Base.

Weave in ends. •

Little Lamb Easter Egg Cozy

Easy

MATERIALS

YARN

LION BRAND® Wool-Ease®, 3oz/85g balls, each approx 197yd/180m (acrylic/wool) (4)

- 1 ball each in #152 Oxford Grey (A), #153 Black (B)
- Small amount of pink yarn

HOOK

- One size G-6 (4 mm)

NOTIONS

- Stitch marker
- Tapestry needle
- Small black beads

GAUGE

Exact gauge is not needed for this project.

NOTE

Work in continuous rnds; do not join or turn unless otherwise instructed.

COZY

With A, ch 2.

Rnd 1 Work 4 sc in first ch. Place marker in first st for beg of rnd; move marker up as each rnd is completed.

Rnd 2 Work 2 sc in each st around—8 sts.

Rnd 3 *2 sc in next st, sc in next st, rep from * around—12 sts.

Rnd 4 *2 sc in next st, sc in each of next 2 sts, rep from * around—16 sts.

Rnd 5 *2 sc in next st, sc in each of next 3 sts, rep from * around—20 sts.

Rnd 6 *2 sc in next st, sc in each of next 4 sts, rep from * around—24 sts.

Rnds 7-14 Sc in each sc around.

Rnd 15 *Sc2tog, sc in each of next 2 sts, rep from * around. Fasten off.

FACE

With B, ch 2.

Rnd 1 Work 6 sc in first ch. Place marker in first st for beg of rnd; move marker up as each rnd is completed.

Rnd 2 Work 2 sc in each st around—12 sts.

Rnd 3 *2 sc in next st, sc in next st, rep from * around—18 sts. Fasten off.

EAR

(Make 2)

With B, ch 2.

Rnd 1 Work 6 sc in first ch. Place marker in first st for beg of rnd; move marker up as each rnd is completed.

Rnd 2 Work 2 sc in each st around—12 sts. Fasten off.

FINISHING

Sew beads to Face for eyes. With pink yarn, embroider a straight st "Y" for nose. Sew Face to Body. Fold Ear circles in half and sew to cozy.

Weave in ends. •

Terry Turtle

Easy

MEASUREMENTS
Approx 2"/5 cm tall

MATERIALS
YARN
LION BRAND® Vanna's Choice®, 3.5oz/100g balls, each approx 170yd/156m (acrylic/rayon)
- 1 ball each in #170 Pea Green (A), #173 Dusty Green (B)

HOOK
- One size G-6 (4 mm)

NOTIONS
- Stitch marker
- Tapestry needle
- 2 plastic safety eyes, 6 mm diameter
- Fiberfill stuffing

GAUGE
Exact gauge is not needed for this project.

NOTE
Work in continuous rnds; do not join or turn unless otherwise instructed.

TURTLE
UPPER SHELL
With A, ch 2.

Rnd 1 Work 6 sc in first ch. Place marker in first st for beg of rnd; move marker up as each rnd is completed.
Rnd 2 2 sc in each sc around—12 sts.
Rnd 3 *2 sc in next sc, sc in next sc; rep from * around—18 sts.
Rnd 4 *2 sc in next sc, sc in next 2 sc; rep from * around—24 sts.
Rnd 5 *2 sc in next sc, sc in next 3 sc; rep from * around—30 sts.
Rnd 6 *2 sc in next sc, sc in next 4 sc; rep from * around—36 sts.
Rnd 7 *2 sc in next sc, sc in next 5 sc; rep from * around—42 sts.
Rnd 8 *2 sc in next sc, sc in next 6 sc; rep from * around—48 sts.
Rnds 9-14 Sc in each sc around.
Fasten off.

BOTTOM SHELL
With B, ch 2.
Rnds 1-8 Work Rnds 1-8 of Upper Shell—48 sts.
Fasten off.

HEAD
With B, ch 2.
Rnd 1 Work 6 sc in first ch. Place marker in first st for beg of rnd; move marker up as each rnd is completed.
Rnd 2 2 sc in each sc around—12 sts.
Rnd 3 2 sc in next sc, sc in next 10 sc, 2 sc in next sc—14 sts.
Rnd 4 2 sc in next sc, sc in next 12 sc, 2 sc in next sc—16 sts.
Rnd 5 2 sc in next sc, sc in next 14 sc, 2 sc in next sc—18 sts.
Rnd 6 Sc in each sc around.
Rnd 7 Sc2tog, sc in next 14 sc, sc2tog—16 sts.
Rnd 8 Sc2tog, sc in next 12 sc, sc2tog—14 sts.
Rnd 9 Sc2tog, sc in next 10 sc, sc2tog—12 sts.
Fasten off.

LEG
(Make 4)
With B, ch 2.
Rnd 1 Work 4 sc in first ch. Place marker in first st for beg of rnd; move marker up as each rnd is completed.
Rnd 2 2 sc in each sc around—8 sts.

Rnds 3-5 Sc in each sc around. Fasten off.

TAIL

With B, ch 2.

Rnd 1 Work 4 sc in first ch. Place marker in first st for beg of rnd; move marker up as each rnd is completed.

Rnds 2-4 Sc in each sc around—4 sts. Fasten off.

FINISHING

Following package directions, attach safety eyes to Head. Stuff Upper Shell and sew to Bottom Shell. Stuff Head and sew to Shell. Stuff Legs and Tail very lightly and sew to Shell.

Weave in ends. •

Florence Flamingo

Easy

MEASUREMENTS
Approx 8"/20.5 cm tall

MATERIALS
YARN
LION BRAND® Feels Like Butta®, 3.5 oz/100 g balls, each approx 55 yd/50 m (polyester) 6
- 1 ball each in #101 Pink (A), #100 White (B), #153 Black (C), #157 Yellow (D)

LION BRAND® Go For Faux®, 3.5 oz/100 g balls, each approx 65 yd/60 m (polyester) 6
- 1 ball in #205 Pink Poodle (E)

HOOKS
- One size F-5 (3.75 mm) and one size H-8 (5 mm)

NOTIONS
- Stitch markers
- Tapestry needle
- 2 safety eyes, 12mm diameter
- Fiberfill stuffing

GAUGE
24 sc and 28 rnds = approx 4"/10 cm with smaller hook and A. See Notes.

NOTES
1) Flamingo is made in 9 pieces: Body/Neck/Head, 2 Eyes, 2 Feet, 2 Legs, and 2 Wings.
2) Pieces are stuffed and then sewn together.
3) Exact gauge isn't crucial but it is meant to be a bit tight—this helps keep the stuffing from poking through.

FLAMINGO
BODY/NECK/HEAD
Beg at back end of Body, with smaller hook and A, ch 2.

Rnd 1 Work 6 sc in second ch from hook. Place marker in first st for beg of rnd; move marker up as each rnd is completed.

Rnds 2, 4, and 6 Sc in each st around.

Rnd 3 Work 2 sc in each st around—12 sc.

Rnd 5 *Sc in next st, 2 sc in next st; rep from * around—18 sc.

Rnd 7 Sc in each st around.

Rnd 8 *Sc in next 2 sts, 2 sc in next st; rep from * around—24 sc.

Rnd 9 Sc in each st around.

Rnd 10 *Sc in next 3 sts, 2 sc in next st; rep from * around—30 sc.

Rnd 11 Sc in each st around.

Rnd 12 *Sc in next 4 sts, 2 sc in next st; rep from * around—36 sc.

Rnd 13 Sc in each st around.

Rnd 14 *Sc in next 5 sts, 2 sc in next st; rep from * around—42 sc.

Rnd 15 Sc in each st around.

Rnd 16 *Sc in next 6 sts, 2 sc in next st; rep from * around—48 sc.

Rnd 17 Sc in each st around.

Rnd 18 *Sc in next 7 sts, 2 sc in next st; rep from * around—54 sc.

Rnd 19 Sc in each st around.

Rnd 20 *Sc in next 8 sts, 2 sc in next st; rep from * around—60 sc.

Rnds 21-47 Sc in each st around.

Rnd 48 *Sc in next 4 sts, sc2tog; rep from * around—50 sc.

Rnd 49 *Sc in next 3 sts, sc2tog; rep from * around—40 sc.

Rnd 50 *Sc in next 2 sts, sc2tog; rep from * around—30 sc.

Place marker in Rnd 50 to indicate where sts will be sewn to shape bottom of Neck.

Stuff Body firmly.

Rnd 51 *Sc in next st, sc2tog; rep from * around—20 sc.

Neck

Note Stuff Neck firmly as your work progresses.

Rnds 52-63 Sc in each st around.

Place marker in Rnd 63 to indicate where sts will be sewn to shape bottom of Neck.

Rnds 64-87 Sc in each st around.

Place marker in Rnd 87 to indicate where sts will be sewn to shape top of Neck.

Rnds 88-93 Sc in each st around.

Bend Neck up and sew marked Rnds 50 and 63 tog with 3 sts to hold Neck in place. Remove markers from Rnds 50 and 63.

Head

Rnd 94 *Sc in next st, 2 sc in next st; rep from * around—30 sc.

Rnd 95 *Sc in next 2 sts, 2 sc in next st; rep from * around—40 sc.

Rnd 96 Sc in each st around.

Place marker in Rnd 96 to indicate where sts will be sewn to shape top of Neck.

Rnds 97-106 Sc in each st around.

Bend top of Neck down and sew marked Rnds 87 and 96 tog with 3 sts to hold Head in place. Remove markers from Rnds 87 and 96.

Rnd 107 *Sc in next 3 sts, sc2tog; rep from * around—32 sc.

Rnd 108 Sc in each st around.

Rnd 109 *Sc in next 2 sts, sc2tog; rep from * around—24 sc.

Rnd 110 Sc in each st around.

Rnd 111 *Sc in next st, sc2tog; rep from * around; join with sl st in first sc of this rnd—16 sc.

Remove end of rnd marker.

Fasten off.

Beak

Note Read Beak instructions carefully. Some rnds are worked continuously but others are worked as joined rnds.

Rnd 112 Join B with sl st in a st of Rnd 111 that is on

Florence Flamingo

underside of Head, ch 1, sc in same st as joining sl st and in each sc around (take care not to work into the joining sl st of Rnd 111); join with sl st in first sc—16 sc.

Rnd 113 Ch 1, sc in each st around; do not join, work in continuous rnds.

Place marker in last st made to indicate end of rnd; move marker up as each rnd is completed.

Rnd 114 Sc in each st around.

Rnd 115 Sc in each st around; join with sl st in first sc of this rnd.

Remove end of rnd marker.

Fasten off.

Rnd 116 Join A with sl st in a st of Rnd 115 that is on underside of Beak, ch 1, sc in same st as joining sl st and in each sc around; join with sl st in first sc of this rnd.

Fasten off.

Rnd 117 Join C with sl st in a st of Rnd 116 that is on underside of Beak, ch 1, sc in same st as joining sl st and in each sc around; join with sl st in first sc of this rnd.

Rnd 118 Ch 1, sc in each st around; join with sl st in first sc.

Stuff Head and Beak firmly.

Rnd 119 Ch 1, *sc in next 2 sts, sc2tog; rep from * around; join with sl st in first sc—12 sc.

Rnds 120 and 121 Ch 1, sc in each st around; join with sl st in first sc.

Rnd 122 Ch 1, (sc2tog) 6 times; join with sl st in first sc 6 sc.

Rnd 123 Ch 1, sc in each st around; join with sl st in first sc.

Fasten off, leaving a long yarn tail for sewing.

Stuff remainder of Beak lightly, leaving last 3 rnds unstuffed.

Thread yarn tail onto needle and sew Rnds 123 and 117 tog to pull Beak downward.

EYE

(Make 2)

With smaller hook and B, ch 2.

Rnd 1 Work 6 sc in second ch from hook; join with sl st in first sc.

Rnd 2 Ch 1, 2 sc in each st around; join with sl st in first sc—12 sc.

Fasten off, leaving a long yarn tail for sewing.

FOOT

(Make 2)

Beg at heel, with smaller hook and D, ch 2.

Rnd 1 Work 4 sc in second ch from hook; do not join, work in continuous rnds. Place marker in last st made to indicate end of rnd; move marker up as each rnd is completed.

Rnds 2 and 3 Sc in each st around.

Rnd 4 Work 2 sc in each st around—8 sc.

Rnd 5 *Sc in next st, 2 sc in next st; rep from * around—12 sc.

Rnd 6 Sc in each st around.

Rnd 7 *Sc in next st, 2 sc in next st; rep from * around—18 sc.

Do not fasten off, do not stuff.

First Toe

Rnd 1 Sc in next 6 sts, leave rem 12 sts unworked for Second and Third Toes; join with sl st in first sc of this rnd—6 sc.

Rnd 2 Ch 1, sc in each st around; do not join, work in continuous rnds. Place marker in last st made to indicate end of rnd; move marker up as each rnd is completed.

Rnds 3-7 Sc in each st around.

Fasten off, leaving a long yarn tail for sewing. Thread yarn tail onto needle, weave through sts of last rnd, and pull to close opening. Knot.

Second Toe

Rnd 1 Join D with sl st in first unworked st following First Toe, ch 1, sc in same st as joining sl st and in next 2 unworked sts, sk next 6 unworked sts for Third Toe, sc in next 3 unworked sts; join with sl st in first sc of this rnd.

Rnds 2-7 Work Rnds 2-7 of First Toe.

Fasten off, leaving a long yarn tail for sewing. Thread yarn tail onto needle, weave through sts of last rnd, and pull to close opening. Knot.

Third Toe
Rnd 1 Join D with sl st in first unworked st following Second Toe, ch 1, sc in same st as joining sl st and in next 5 unworked sts; join with sl st in first sc of this rnd.
Rnds 2-7 Work Rnds 2-7 of First Toe.
Fasten off, leaving a long yarn tail for sewing. Thread yarn tail onto needle, weave through sts of last rnd, and pull to close opening. Knot.

LEG
(Make 2)
With smaller hook and D, ch 11.
Rnd 1 Sc in second ch from hook and in each ch across; join with sl st in first sc to begin working in rnds—10 sc.
Rnd 2 Ch 1, sc in each st around; do not join, work in continuous rnds. Place marker in last st made to indicate end of rnd; move marker up as each rnd is completed.
Rnds 3-28 Sc in each st around.

Knee
Rnd 29 Work 2 sc in each st around—20 sc.
Rnds 30 and 31 Sc in each st around.
Rnd 32 (Sc2tog) 10 times—10 sc.
Stuff Knee only.
Rnds 33-60 Sc in each st around.
Fasten off, leaving a long yarn tail for sewing. Thread yarn tail onto needle, weave through sts of last rnd, and pull to close opening. Knot.

WING
(Make 2)
With larger hook and E, ch 4.
Row 1 Work 2 dc in fourth ch from hook (3 skipped ch count as dc)—3 dc.
Row 2 Ch 3 (counts as dc), turn, dc in first st (inc made), dc in next st, 2 dc in top of beg ch-3—5 dc.
Row 3 Ch 3 (counts as dc), turn, sk first st, dc in next st, 2 dc in next st, dc in next st, dc in top of beg ch-3—6 dc.
Row 4 Ch 3 (counts as dc), turn, dc in first st, dc in next 4 sts, 2 dc in top of beg ch-3—8 dc.
Row 5 Ch 3 (counts as dc), turn, dc in first st, dc in next 2 sts, 2 dc in next 2 sts, dc in next 2 sts, 2 dc in top of beg ch-3—12 dc.
Row 6 Ch 3 (counts as dc), turn, dc in first st, dc in next 4 sts, 2 dc in next 2 sts, dc in next 4 sts, 2 dc in top of beg ch-3—16 dc.
Row 7 Ch 3 (counts as dc), turn, sk first dc, dc in each st across working last dc in top of beg ch-3.
Row 8 Ch 3 (counts as dc), turn, sk first 2 sts, dc in next 12 sts, sk next st, dc in top of beg ch-3—14 dc.
Row 9 Ch 3 (counts as dc), turn, sk first 2 sts, dc in next 10 sts, sk next st, dc in top of beg ch-3—12 dc.
Row 10 Ch 3 (counts as dc), turn, sk first 2 sts, dc in next 8 sts, sk next st, dc in top of beg ch-3—10 dc.
Row 11 Ch 3 (counts as dc), turn, sk first 2 sts, dc in next 6 sts, sk next st, dc in top of beg ch-3—8 dc.
Row 12 Turn, sc2tog, sc in next 4 sts, sc2tog (working over last dc and beg ch-3)—6 sc.
Row 13 Turn, sc2tog, sc in next 2 sts, sc2tog—4 sc.
Fasten off.

FINISHING
Following package directions, attach safety eye to center of each Eye. Sew Eyes to Head above Beak.
Sew Legs to Flamingo.
Sew Wings to Body, lining up last row of Wing with Neck and overlapping top edges of Wings over back of Flamingo. Leave lower edge of each Wing unsewn so it moves freely.
Weave in ends.

Graduation Bear

Easy

MEASUREMENTS
Approx 6 ½"/16.5 cm tall

MATERIALS
YARN
LION BRAND® Vanna's Choice®, 3.5oz/100g balls, each approx 170yd/156m (acrylic/rayon) **(4)**
- 1 ball each in #123 Beige (A), #109 Colonial Blue (B), #100 White (C)
- Small amounts of brown, yellow, and red yarn

HOOK
- One size G-6 (4 mm)

NOTIONS
- Stitch marker
- Tapestry needle
- 2 plastic safety eyes, 9 mm diameter
- Fiberfill stuffing

GAUGE
Exact gauge is not needed for this project.

NOTE
Work in continuous rnds; do not join rnds or turn unless otherwise instructed.

BEAR
HEAD AND BODY
Beg at top of head, with A, ch 2.

Rnd 1 Work 6 sc in first ch. Place marker in first st for beg of rnd; move marker up as each rnd is completed.

Rnd 2 2 sc in each st around—12 sts.

Rnd 3 *2 sc in next st, sc in next st; rep from * around—18 sts.

Rnd 4 *2 sc in next st, sc in next 2 sts; rep from * around—24 sts.

Rnd 5 *2 sc in next st, sc in next 3 sts; rep from * around—30 sts.

Rnd 6 *2 sc in next st, sc in next 4 sts; rep from * around—36 sts.

Rnds 7-14 Sc in each st around.

Rnd 15 *Sc2tog, sc in next 4 sts; rep from * around—30 sts.

Rnd 16 *Sc2tog, sc in next 3 sts; rep from * around—24 sts.

Rnd 17 *Sc2tog, sc in next 2 sts; rep from * around—18 sts.

Following package instructions, attach safety eyes to face. Start stuffing firmly. Continue stuffing as you go.

Rnds 18-20 Rep Rnds 4-6—36 sts.

Rnds 21-32 Sc in each st around.

Rnds 33-35 Rep Rnds 15-17—18 sts.

Rnd 36 *Sc2tog, sc in next st; rep from * around—12 sts.

Rnd 37 (Sc2tog) 6 times—6 sts.

Fasten off.

ARM
(Make 2)

With A, ch 2.

Rnds 1-3 Work Rnds 1-3 of Head and Body—18 sts.

Rnds 4 and 5 Sc in each st around.

Rnd 6 Sc in next 7 sts, (sc2tog) twice, sc in next 7 sts—16 sts.

Rnd 7 Sc in next 6 sts, (sc2tog) twice, sc in next 6 sts—14 sts.

Rnds 8-12 Sc in each st around.

Rnd 13 (Sc2tog) 7 times—7 sts.

Fasten off.

LEG
(Make 2)

With A, ch 2.

Rnds 1-4 Work Rnds 1-4 of Head and Body—24 sts.

Rnds 5 and 6 Sc in each st around.
Rnd 7 (Sc2tog) 8 times, sc in last 8 sts—16 sts.
Rnds 8-12 Sc in each st around.
Fasten off.

EAR
(Make 1)
With A, ch 2.
Rnds 1-3 Work Rnds 1-3 of Head and Body—18 sts.
Rnds 4 and 5 Sc in each st around.
Rnd 6 (Sc2tog) 9 times—9 sts.
Fasten off.

CAP
With B, ch 2.
Rnds 1-4 Work Rnds 1-4 of Head and Body—24 sts.
Rnd 5 Sc in each st around.
Fasten off.

MORTARBOARD
(Make 2)
With B, ch 13.
Row 1 Sc in second ch from hook and in each ch across—12 sts.
Rows 2-12 Ch 1, turn, sc in each st across.
Fasten off.

DIPLOMA
With C, ch 7.
Row 1 Sc in second ch from hook and in each ch across—6 sts.
Rows 2-5 Ch 1, turn, sc in each st across.
Fasten off.

FINISHING
Stuff Arms and Legs and sew to Body.
With scrap of brown yarn, embroider nose.
With WS of 2 Mortarboard pieces tog and working through both thicknesses, join B with sc in edge and work sc evenly spaced around, working 3 sc in each corner. Sew bottom of Mortarboard to center of Cap and sew Cap onto one side of Head. Sew strand of yellow yarn to center top of Mortarboard (for tassel), fray end of strand. With B, make a French knot on center top of Mortarboard.
Sew Ear to other side of Head.
Roll Diploma and tie with scrap of red yarn. Sew Diploma to one Arm.
Weave in ends. •

Heather the Hippo

Easy

MEASUREMENTS
Approx 8"/20.5 cm tall

MATERIALS
YARN
LION BRAND® Wool-Ease®, 3oz/85g balls, each approx 197yd/180m (acrylic/wool) (4)
- 1 ball each in #191 Violet (A), #195 Azalea Pink (B), #129 Cocoa (small amount) (C), #196 Zinnia (small amount) (D)

HOOKS
- One size F-5 (3.75 mm) and one size H-8 (5 mm)

NOTIONS
- Stitch marker
- Tapestry needle
- Fiberfill stuffing

GAUGE
17 sts + 17 rows with larger hook = 4"/10 cm in sc.
Exact gauge is not needed for this project.

NOTE
Work in continuous rnds; do not join or turn unless otherwise instructed.

HIPPO
HEAD
With larger hook and A, ch 3; join with sl st in first ch to form ring.

Rnd 1 Work 6 sc in ring; do not join. Place marker in first st for beg of rnd; move marker up as each rnd is completed.
Rnd 2 2 sc in each sc around—12 sts.
Rnd 3 (Sc in next sc, 2 sc in next sc) around—18 sts.
Rnd 4 (Sc in next 2 sc, 2 sc in next sc) around—24 sts.
Rnd 5 (Sc in next 3 sc, 2 sc in next sc) around—30 sts.
Rnds 6-8 Sc in each sc around.
Rnd 9 (Sc in next 3 sc, sc2tog) around—24 sts.
Rnds 10 and 11 Sc in each sc around.
Rnd 12 (Sc in next 3 sc, 2 sc in next sc) around—30 sts.
Rnds 13 and 14 Sc in each sc around.
Rnd 15 (Sc in next 4 sc, 2 sc in next sc) around—36 sts.
Rnds 16-20 Sc in each sc around.
Rnd 21 (Sc in next sc, sc2tog) 12 times—24 sts.
Stuff Head with fiberfill.
Rnd 22 (Sc in next sc, sc2tog) 8 times—16 sts.
Rnd 23 Sc in each sc around.
Rnd 24 (Sc2tog) 8 times—8 sts.
Fasten off, leaving a long tail. Weave tail through sts of last rnd, gather tog and knot. Leave long tail for sewing.

BODY
Note Worked from neck down.
With larger hook and A, ch 3; join with sl st in first ch to form ring.
Rnd 1 Work 6 sc in ring; do not join. Place marker in first st for beg of rnd; move marker as each rnd is completed.
Rnd 2 2 sc in each sc around—12 sts.
Rnd 3 Sc in each sc around.
Rnd 4 (Sc in next sc, 2 sc in next sc) around—18 sts.
Rnd 5 (Sc in next 2 sc, 2 sc in next sc) around—24 sts.
Rnd 6 (Sc in next 3 sc, 2 sc in next sc) around—30 sts.
Rnd 7 (Sc in next 4 sc, 2 sc in next sc) around—36 sts.
Rnds 8-13 Sc in each sc around.
Rnd 14 (Sc in next 4 sc, sc2tog) around—30 sts.
Rnds 15 and 16 Sc in each sc around.
Rnd 17 (Sc in next 4 sc, 2 sc in next sc) around—36 sts.
Rnd 18 Sc in each sc around.
Rnd 19 (Sc in next 5 sc, 2 sc in next sc) around—42 sts.
Rnds 20-26 Sc in each sc around.

Heather the Hippo

Rnd 27 (Sc in next 5 sc, sc2tog) around—36 sts.

Rnd 28 (Sc in next sc, sc2tog) 12 times—24 sts.

Stuff Body with fiberfill.

Rnd 29 (Sc in next 2 sc, sc2tog) around—18 sts.

Rnd 30 Sc in each sc around.

Rnd 31 (Sc2tog) 9 times—9 sts.

Fasten off, leaving a long tail. Weave tail through sts of last rnd, gather tog, and knot. Leave long tail for sewing.

BACK LEG

(Make 2)

With larger hook and A, ch 3; join with sl st in first ch to form ring.

Rnd 1 Work 6 sc in ring; do not join. Place marker in first st for beg of rnd; move marker up as each rnd is completed.

Rnd 2 2 sc in each sc around—12 sts.

Rnd 3 (Sc in next sc, 2 sc in next sc) around—18 sts.

Rnd 4 (Sc in next 5 sc, 2 sc in next sc) around—21 sts.

Rnd 5 *Working in back loops only,* sc in each sc around.

Rnds 6 and 7 Sc in each sc around.

Rnd 8 (Sc in next 5 sc, sc2tog) around—18 sts.

Rnds 9-12 Sc in each sc around.

Change to working in rows.

Row 13 Sc in next 4 sc; leave rem sts unworked.

Row 14 Ch 1, turn, sc in first 4 sc, 2 sc in next sc, sc in next 4 sc; leave rem sts unworked—10 sts.

Row 15 Ch 1, turn, sc in first 9 sc; leave last sc unworked.

Row 16 Ch 1, turn, sc in first 8 sc; leave last sc unworked.

Row 17 Ch 1, turn, sc in first 3 sc, 2 sc in next sc, sc in next 3 sc; leave last sc unworked—8 sts.

Row 18 Ch 1, turn, sc in first 7 sc; leave last sc unworked.

Row 19 Ch 1, turn, sc in first 6 sc; leave last sc unworked.

Row 20 Ch 1, turn, sc in first 2 sc, 2 sc in next sc, sc in next 2 sc; leave last sc unworked—6 sts.

Rnd 21 Ch 1, turn, work 21 sc evenly spaced around, join with sl st in first sc.

Fasten off, leaving a long tail for sewing.

FRONT LEG

(Make 2)

With larger hook and A, ch 3; join with sl st in first ch to form ring.

Rnd 1 Work 6 sc in ring; do not join. Place marker in first st for beg of rnd; move marker up as each rnd is completed.

Rnd 2 Work 2 sc in each sc around—12 sts.

Rnd 3 (Sc in next sc, 2 sc in next sc) around—18 sts.

Rnd 4 *Working in back loops only,* sc in each sc around.

Rnds 5-12 Sc in each sc around.

Change to working in rows.

Rows 13-20 Work as for Rows 13-20 of Back Leg.

Rnd 21 Ch 1, turn, work 21 sc evenly spaced around, join with sl st in first sc.

Fasten off, leaving a long tail for sewing.

EAR

(Make 2)

With larger hook and A, ch 3.

Row 1 Sc in second ch from hook and in next ch—2 sts.

Row 2 Ch 1, turn, sc in each sc across.

Row 3 Ch 1, turn, 2 sc in each sc—4 sts.

Row 4 Ch 1, turn, (sc2tog) twice—2 sts.

Row 5 Ch 1, turn, sc2tog—1 sts.

Fasten off. Fold Ear in half along Row 1.

Edging

Join A with sl st at Row 1 and sc through both thicknesses; working through single thickness, sc evenly around edge of Ear.

Fasten off.

FINISHING

Sew Head to Body. Stuff Legs and sew to Body. Sew Ears to Head.

With C, embroider straight st eyes and nostrils.

With D, embroider straight st mouth.

Weave in ends.

BIKINI

BIKINI TOP

With smaller hook and B, ch 43.

Row 1 Sc in second ch from hook and in each ch across—42 sts.

Row 2 Ch 1, turn. Rep Row 1.

Fasten off.

BIKINI BOTTOM

Ruffle

With smaller hook and B, ch 34.

Row 1 Sc in second ch from hook and in each ch across—33 sts.

Row 2 Ch 2, turn. Hdc in each st across.

Row 3 Ch 2, turn. Work 4 hdc in first st, *work 5 hdc in next st, rep from * across.

Fasten off.

Center Strip

With smaller hook and B, ch 10.

Row 1 Sc in second ch from hook and in each ch across—9 sts.

Row 2 Ch 1, turn. Sc in each st across.

Rep Row 2 until piece measures 6.5"/16.5 cm from beginning.

Fasten off.

FINISHING

Top

With smaller hook and B, make a ch about 15"/38 cm long. Fasten off.

Weave ch through edge of Top, at center of Row 2. Tie ch around Hippo's neck, tie ends of Top at Body back. Weave in ends.

Bottom

Sew Center Strip to center of Ruffle strip, behind Row 3. Wrap Center Strip to Hippo back and sew in place. Sew ends of Ruffle together at Hippo back.

Weave in ends. ●

Bon-Bon Magnets

Easy

MEASUREMENTS
Approx 1 3/8"/3.5 cm across

MATERIALS
YARN
LION BRAND® Vanna's Choice®, 3.5oz/100g balls, each approx 170yd/156m (acrylic/rayon)
• 1 ball each in #126 Chocolate (A), #100 White (B), #101 Pink (C)

HOOK
• One size H-8 (5 mm)

NOTIONS
• Stitch marker
• Tapestry needle
• Fiberfill stuffing
• Small magnets
• Craft glue

GAUGE
Exact gauge is not needed for this project.

NOTE
Work in continuous rnds; do not join or turn unless otherwise instructed.

BON-BON
(Make 3, 1 each with A, B, and C)
With A, ch 2.
Rnd 1 Work 6 sc in first ch. Place marker in first st for beg of rnd; move marker up as each rnd is completed.
Rnd 2 Work 2 sc in each st around—12 sts.
Rnd 3 *2 sc in next st, sc in next st, rep from * around—18 sts.
Rnds 4-6 Sc in each sc around.
Stuff firmly.
Rnd 7 *Working through back loops only,* *sc2tog, sc in next st, rep from * around—12 sts.
Rnd 8 (Sc2tog) around—6 sts.
Fasten off.

FINISHING
Cut lengths of each yarn. Use contrast colors to make zigzags, drizzles, or spirals, glue to top of Bon-Bons. Glue magnet to back of each Bon-Bon. Weave in ends. •